PARTY WITH A PURPOSE

PUBLISHING

The Prospecting, Production,
& Personal Growth People

Party with a Purpose
by Pat Pearson

Printed in United States of America
First edition July 2005

ISBN: 1-891279-14-9
Published by INTI Publishing, a division of INTI, Inc.
intipublishing.com

Quantity discounts available
Inquiries should be addressed to:

INTI Publishing, Inc.
6704 Benjamin Rd., Suite 500
Tampa, FL 33634
(813) 881-1638
intipublishing.com

Cover design and text layout by Parry Design Studio

PARTY
WITH A
PURPOSE

Pat Pearson, M.S.S.W.

About INTI

Founded in 1990, INTI, Inc. operates two divisions to support the two biggest challenges in the industry — recruiting and retention.

INTI's Recruiting Division educates and enlightens prospects about the Direct Sales industry through a variety of content-rich books, CDs, and DVDs. To date, INTI's books have sold more than five million copies and been translated into 25 languages. INTI can customize its messages for individual companies and offers complete turnkey solutions, including design, production, and duplication services.

INTI's Retention Division stresses an "edu-tainment" approach to training and support by offering a host of captivating speakers available through the INTI Speaker's Bureau. In addition, INTI warehouses more than 600 book titles at discount prices and features a Women's Bookstore with hundreds of titles covering a wide range of women's issues, available online at **intipublishing.com**. INTI also offers a Monthly Mentoring series hosted by Pat Pearson, a highly respected psychotherapist and author of *Party with a Purpose*.

INTI's client list includes a host of Party Plan, Network Marketing, and Direct Sales companies. For more information about INTI's wide-range of services or to book Pat Pearson or another speaker for your next event, call INTI, Inc. **(813) 881-1638.**

Dedication

To the man who keeps me laughing, going, and balanced. The funniest, kindest man I know... my husband, Steve Frohling.

Acknowledgment

So many people... have you ever thought of all the lives that we touch? In Direct Selling, it's literally thousands and thousands of people and families.

This book owes its life to these people and their personal struggles for excellence. I've coached, laughed with, and cried with thousands of people who know that how they run their lives is how they run their business. We've worked together to make both areas grow and prosper. This book takes all the wisdom of how to do that and brings it to your world.

The truth is, if you stay in your business long enough and work at it hard enough, you will be successful.

The question is: how long is it taking and how much do you have to endure? This book will help you achieve the psychological breakthroughs you need to speed up that process.

First and foremost, I want to acknowledge INTI Publishing and its dynamic duo of Katherine Glover and Steve Price. I thank you for your courage to take the risk for new material and your ongoing support for me and my work.

For Steve Price: I've never worked more easily with someone. Your great sense of humor and insight has made writing this book a joy.

For Katherine Glover: You're a delight to know and work with. You truly inspire me to have more fun and make more money! Your vision is extraordinary and points us all towards a positive future.

For Debbie Cortes: You're the wonderful connector that makes everything work. Thank you for your patience and diligence.

From my office of Pearson Presentations... there is the queen of everything, Stephanie Destatte. You're the most capable and biggest-hearted person I know. Thank you for putting up with the chaos. Your good humor and "can-do" attitude makes it all work!

Last, but never least, for Steve Frohling, my best friend, husband, and love: Thank you for being by my side through it all. I wish us more joy and many more memorable experiences together.

Foreword

I'm blessed, no doubt about it.

I travel the globe giving speeches and conducting seminars on the psychology of success in Direct Sales. Visiting great cities while impacting the lives of thousands of women each year — talk about a dream job!

The only downside is I don't have enough time in a one-hour speech or half-day seminar to share all of the knowledge I've accumulated during my experiences — first, as a clinical psychotherapist, and for the past 20-plus years, as a consultant and coach to Direct Sales professionals.

That's why I wrote *Party with a Purpose* — to provide you with a "psychological reference guide" that will help you identify and deal with the key emotional issues everyone in this business must face.

If you've heard me speak, or if you've read one of my previous books, you'll likely recognize some of the material contained in these pages, such as the chapters on "Stopping Self Sabotage" and "Refusing a Ride on the Rescue Triangle." Be sure to read these chapters again, as I have reshaped the material to apply to the two biggest psychological challenges in the business — recruiting and retention.

I've also included plenty of new material in this book, including facts and figures about the industry and research on why women are psychologically suited to succeed in the Party Plan concept.

This book is designed to help you negotiate the emotional roadblocks that you and your people will face in your business. Your biggest challenge in the business doesn't involve the products or the opportunity. Your biggest challenge involves people — understanding people... motivating people... managing people... teaching people... mentoring people... and leading people.

The Party Plan concept is a fun business. A purpose-driven business. But first and foremost, a people business. The more you understand the psychology of this business, the better you'll be at building yourself, building your people, and building your business. Think of this book as a crash course in the psychology of success. Once you learn and apply the information in this book and then teach it to your teammates, your business will flourish like never before.

Wishing you all the success you deserve,

Pat

TABLE OF CONTENTS

INTRODUCTION

The Psychology of Success in Party Plan Marketing

*When we face our own fears and practice
the techniques of change, we can stop sabotaging
all our hopes and dreams.*

**Pat Pearson
from Stop Self-Sabotage!**

Why write a book about the psychology behind Party Plan Marketing? My motivation can be summed up by Yogi Berra's oft-quoted observation about baseball:

"The physical part of the game is 90% mental."

Okay, Yogi's syntax is tangled, but his intended insight still rings true: In sports, success depends more on a strong mind than a strong body. The same can be said for the Party Plan business concept — success is 90% mental.

Have you ever wondered why some women in the business become wildly successful, while others involved with the same company drop out of the business within weeks or months of signing up?

3

The answer lies in what I call the "POP Theory." The first **P** stands for the **product**. The **O** stands for the **opportunity**. And the final **P** stands for **people.**

POP Theory

P roduct
O pportunity
P eople

Within six months of joining a Party Plan company, everybody is familiar with the **Product** line and understands the **Opportunity.** So, if everybody is on equal footing with the product and opportunity at the six-month point, why is it that some women's businesses take off, while others drop out?

The answer is **People**, the third P in the POP Theory. People. That's where the biggest challenge in the business stems from — those walking, talking, *feeling* packages of protoplasm that we call people. Like every aspect of life, people's emotions play a big part in the business. People buy into the business on an emotional high... and they buy out of the business on an emotional low. To become successful in this business, then, you must learn how to *manage your emotions while teaching others proven strategies* to deal with their emotional issues.

> *People buy into the business on an emotional high... and they buy out of the business on an emotional low.*

The key to success and longevity in Party Plan Marketing is your ability to recruit and retain good people. Sounds simple enough. But because the business you're in is a **people business...** and because people are emotional beings, you need to be able to "get inside people's heads" so you can better motivate and manage them.

> *"If you're in this business six months or longer, then you're a practicing psychologist, whether you're trained or not!"*

As a 30-year veteran put it, *"If you're in this business six months or longer, then you're a practicing psychologist, whether you're trained or not!"*

You're a Sounding Board for People's Problems

Party Plan Marketing is a simple business.

Simple, yes. Easy, no.

It's *simple* because you can learn everything you need to learn about the products and the opportunity in a few weeks. But it's *not easy* because dealing with people is never easy, and this business is — first, last, and foremost — **a people business!** What separates the top leaders and producers from the wanna-be's is the ability to deal with people.

A big part of your job is to listen to people's stories. People will call you to discuss the emotional issues that are troubling them. If they're upset with their husband, they'll call. If one of their kids gets in trouble at school, you'll hear about it. A good leader understands that a big part of team building is *caring for* and *counseling* your people.

There's an old expression that rings true in this business: *No one cares how much you know until they know how much you care.* In other words, in this business, how much you **care about people** counts for more than **how much you know about the product and opportunity.**

For every emotional breakthrough or insight, production goes up 25%.

"Choosing the What" vs. "Choosing the Who"

It's been my observation that 20% to 40% of your success depends on **"choosing the what,"** that is, choosing WHAT you know about the product and opportunity; whereas 60% to 80% of success depends on **"choosing the who,"** that is, choosing WHO you recruit, WHO you mentor, and WHO you give your time to.

In the final analysis, the leaders who invest most of their time and efforts in their people are the ones who will build the biggest, most productive teams. I can't emphasize enough the psychological aspect of this business. It's been my observation that for every emotional breakthrough or insight, production goes up 25%. That's why it's crucial for you to understand the emotional issues that have the biggest impact on you and your people.

Since "you're a practicing psychologist whether you're trained or not," doesn't it make sense to get some training that will help you help your people? Sure does — and that's exactly what this book is designed to do.

My Background as a Psychotherapist

I've had 25 years of experience as a clinical psychotherapist; since 1985, I've concentrated on helping people in Direct Sales achieve their full potential in their personal and professional lives by teaching them to replace self-defeating behaviors with positive, productive ones.

I got involved with the Party Plan industry quite by accident. I was working as a clinical therapist when a friend asked me to talk to a group of business leaders who, in my friend's opinion, weren't performing up to their potential.

I put together a two-hour seminar to help the participants move past self-sabotaging behaviors and create more success in their lives. The seminar was so well received that I was asked to give another... and another... until the demand became so strong that I decided to devote my time exclusively to teaching Direct Sales professionals the psychological strategies for success.

Why I Wrote This Book

I wrote this book to help Party Plan professionals identify the emotional roadblocks that detour them and their people on their road to success. I designed this book to help everyone in this industry, from the prospect who wants to learn more about the business... to the brand-new recruit who signed up yesterday... to the struggling veteran who isn't getting the results she wants... to the long-time leader who has built a large, profitable organization.

Ninety percent of recruiting and retention is mental. That's why understanding and managing the psychological aspects of the business is indispensable to your success.

Success in this business is a one-two punch — **recruiting** and **retention.** To grow your business to its fullest potential, you have to *get people in* your business, and you have to *keep them in* the business. If you're good at both phases, then you're destined for more success than you ever dreamed possible.

But as I pointed out earlier, 90% of recruiting and retention is mental. That's why understanding and managing the psychological aspects of the business is indispensable to your success.

What This Book Will Do for You

It stands to reason that if the biggest challenges in the business are psychological, then the solutions are psychological. In the end, the people who will benefit most from this book are the women who need help in dealing with the emotional issues that keep sidetracking their businesses and their lives. In other words, *you and everyone in your organization!*

How you run your life is how you run your business. When you learn how to run your life better, your business will follow.

Your biggest frustration in this business comes from dealing with people. Once you understand the psychological issues in the business, and once you learn the strategies to manage those issues, then you'll be able to reduce your frustration and your stress by helping yourself and everyone else in your group.

The information you're about to learn is customized for the Direct Sales industry, but it applies to all phases of life. The strategies in this book will help you improve all of your relationships, including the ones with your spouse, your children, your friends, and your family. As I tell my audiences, **How you run your life is how you run your business. When you learn how to run your life better, your business will follow.**

Be forewarned. Dealing with emotional issues is an ongoing process, not a one-time event. Think of yourself as a counselor on call, and think of this book as a psychological reference guide that will enable you and your people to recognize and manage the key emotional issues that everyone in this business has to deal with.

Never Lose Sight of Your Purpose!

When was the last time you took a few minutes to reflect on your purpose in getting involved in the business?

Was your purpose to help others by sharing the products and the opportunity?

Was your purpose to enjoy the companionship of like-minded women?

Was your purpose to grow as a person and support others in their personal growth?

Was your purpose to earn extra income while working a flexible schedule?

Was your purpose to pay off credit card debt or add to the kids' college fund?

Or was your purpose to control your destiny by owning your own potentially high-profit home-based business?

No matter what your purpose, it can be accomplished through the Party Plan concept, a dynamic, growing industry with a bright future.

Your purpose is yours and yours alone, so don't take it lightly! Embrace your purpose. Own it. And use it as a beacon to light your way during the dark times.

> *Embrace your purpose. Own it. And use it as a beacon to light your way during the dark times.*

My purpose in writing this book is to give you proven psychological strategies that will help you realize your dreams in the business.

By combining my strategies with your commitment, your future is sure to become one long party — a *Party with a Purpose.*

PARTY WITH A PURPOSE

Party Plans:
A Horse of a Different Color

To love what you do and feel that it matters —
how could anything be more fun?

Katharine Graham
Publisher, *The Washington Post*

R emember the scene from the *Wizard of Oz* where Dorothy and her companions finally enter the Emerald City and are taken for a carriage ride pulled by "a horse of a different color?" Remember how the horse literally changed colors as it trotted along?

When compared to other horses, that "horse of a different color" was certainly unique looking, wasn't it? Made you light up and smile, didn't it? But when you think about it, the horse of a different color did what *all* carriage horses are designed to do — it delivered passengers to their destination.

Well, the same can be said of the Party Plan business concept. Compared to traditional businesses, this business is a horse of a different color, but it can still deliver you to your destination, wherever that may be — and you'll have a lot more fun in the process.

Compared to traditional businesses, this business is a horse of a different color, but it can still deliver you to your destination, wherever that may be.

For millions of women, the Party Plan horse and carriage is just the right vehicle to take them where they want to go. And it can deliver you to your destination, too. You're the driver, so it's up to you to set the pace and steer the carriage.

A Word About This Unique and Growing Industry

Although the focus of this book is on the psychology behind recruiting and retention of Party Plan partners, I'd be remiss if I didn't talk about how the Party Plan concept came into being and where the industry is headed.

Most likely you were attracted to the business by the product or the opportunity or both, which happens a lot because Party Plan companies offer one-of-a-kind, top-quality products that aren't available in retail stores.

But before we get into the psychology of success, I think it will be helpful for you to know some crucial facts about this vibrant, 75-year-old industry so that you'll better understand why it's attracting so much attention from women looking for a non-traditional business opportunity, as well as multi-national corporations and Wall Street investors who are impressed by the industry's steady growth and bright future.

The following information will serve to further validate your decision to sign up as a Party Plan partner, or, if you're already involved, will strengthen your resolve to make the most out of an opportunity that is redefining the way the world works and shops.

Going Against the Marketing Grain

If you've ever wondered how the Party Plan concept came about, here is a brief history of the evolution of the industry. Prior to huge department stores and mega-malls, door-to-door selling accounted for a large part of retailing in this country. Thousands of traveling salesmen spent much of their lives on the road, lugging their encyclopedias, sewing machines, and pots and pans from one house to another.

In the 1930s, Frank Beveridge, the president of a door-to-door cleaning supplies company, noticed that one of his salesmen was making record-breaking sales by demonstrating the products at home parties held in the living rooms of neighborhood hostesses. Beveridge immediately recognized that informal gatherings in people's homes could rapidly take his business to a whole new level, and by 1940, he had transformed his company into the first strictly Party Plan sales and marketing concept.

Today, nearly 75 years after a door-to-door salesman initiated the first home party, the industry is dominated by the very audience it serves — women.

As a result of the shift to home parties, more and more women began to discover that Party Plans were a convenient, flexible way to have fun and help others, while supplementing the family income.

Today, nearly 75 years after a door-to-door salesman initiated the first home party, the industry is dominated by the very audience it serves — women.

Not Your Grandmother's Party Plan Concept

The Party Plan concept has come a long way since the 1940s — and, with improved communication devices and millions more women in the workplace, the industry is just now entering its peak growth period.

The Party Plan method is by far the fastest growing segment of the Direct Sales industry.

The facts tell the tale: In 2004, Direct Selling accounted for more than $30 billion in sales, double the sales of the previous decade, and during that 10-year period, the Party Plan method was by far the fastest growing segment of the Direct Sales industry.

According to the Direct Selling Association, 100-plus Party Plan companies are members in good standing, and the membership role continues to expand yearly. Today there are 13 million people working in Direct Sales, almost 80% of whom are women. And in the Party Plan segment, women are even more dominant, making up an astonishing 99% of the sales force.

Today there are 13 million people working in Direct Sales, almost 80% of whom are women. And in the Party Plan segment, women are even more dominant, making up an astonishing 99% of the sales force.

Many Party Plan companies routinely report annual earnings of $100 million or more, and for the last five years, the Direct Sales industry has enjoyed nearly double digit growth during a time when the majority of traditional retailers were reporting lower than expected sales.

Little wonder, then, that the Party Plan concept has gotten the financial backing of mega investors and giant corporations. Warren Buffett, the world's second richest man, owns two Party Plan companies, and several forward-looking Fortune 500 companies have followed the trend by adding Party Plan divisions to their marketing mix.

Although each company has its own particular style of marketing, Party Plans generally follow a system that empowers women all over the world to have fun... help others... and make money.

Today, there are literally millions of women working with hundreds of companies distributing thousands of products using the Party Plan method of sales and marketing. Although each company has its own particular style of marketing, Party Plans generally follow a system that empowers women all over the world to have fun... help others... and make money.

"The Five P's" of Party Plan

During my years as a consultant to the Direct Sales industry, I've interviewed thousands of women to discover the key psychological reasons they joined the business. The reasons fall into five categories that I call "The Five P's." Here, in no particular order, are the main reasons women are drawn to the business:

The Five P's
1. People
2. Purpose
3. Personal Growth
4. Passion
5. Profit

Let's take a few moments to examine each of the Five P's in more detail.

1. **People:** Humans are social animals, so we seek opportunities to gather in groups to share, laugh, talk, encourage, buy, and so on. Many women love the people side of the business because they enjoy not only the friendly interaction, but also the opportunity to help others.

2. **Purpose:** Because Party Plan companies have a positive corporate culture and stress durable family values, participants are encouraged to live centered, purpose-driven lives. As the old saying goes, "You have to stand for something, or you'll fall for anything," and the Party Plan opportunity can help you re-focus and re-energize your purpose.

3. **Personal Growth:** The Party Plan business concept stimulates personal growth. More often than not, all that people need in order to blossom is the right mentor to encourage them... or the right challenge to fire them up... so that they move out of their old comfort zone and grow into fully actualized humans.

4. **Passion:** It's easy to get caught in a rut, worn down and worn out by the same old routines. That's why it's crucial to find something you're passionate about. Passion restores your vitality and energizes your life. Being in the business forces you out of your routines and offers you the opportunity to feel passionate about the products, as well as the opportunity to help yourself, your family, and other women.

5. **Profit:** True, the best things in life are free — love, friends, and family, for example. But *money gives us the freedom and the opportunity to enjoy those things* **when** we choose... **as often** as we choose... and **where** we choose. The business allows people to make money while making a difference in people's lives. It doesn't get any better than that.

There you have it — the Five P's — the five psychological reasons women choose to become Party Plan participants. Add to these the flexibility of setting your own hours and the rewards of owning your own business, and it's easy to see why millions of women are partnering with hundreds of Party Plan companies around the globe.

Party Plan companies love women! Why? Because females are ideally suited for this unique business concept.

Yes, it's easy to see why women love Party Plan companies. And the feeling is mutual — *Party Plan companies love women!* Why? Because females are ideally suited for this unique business concept. Not only does the business concept break the rules of traditional business, but also, *Party Plan companies break the glass ceiling!* (All I can say is, "It's about time!")

So, let's turn the page to learn why women are ideally suited for the Party Plan method of sales and marketing.

CHAPTER TWO 2

Women Are From Venus — the Party Plan Planet

Not only do men and women communicate differently, but they think, feel, perceive, react, respond, love, need, and appreciate differently. They almost seem to be from different planets, speaking different languages, and needing different nourishment.

John Gray, Ph.D.
Men Are from Mars, Women Are from Venus

Not long ago I heard a speech by Dr. Phil in which he summed up one of the biggest differences between men and women with this observation:

"Women speak 4,500 to 5,000 words a day. Men, on the other hand, only speak 1,500 words — and 1,494 of them are spoken *before* they get home. The only six words men use at home are *'Seen the remote?'* and *'What's for dinner?'*"

The women in the audience howled with laughter. A few men laughed, but most had a bewildered look on their face that said, "I don't get it."

My purpose in telling you this story is *not* to bash men, but to point out one of the major documented differences between men and women: Women literally talk three to four times more than men. That's not a joke. That's a fact.

Note — the fact that women are more verbal than men doesn't make men "wrong" and women "right." *But it does make women better suited and more adept at certain tasks.* More to the point, women's verbal skills (as well as some other key traits we'll talk about in this chapter) make them more psychologically suited to the Party Plan concept.

> *More to the point, women's verbal skills, as well as some other key traits, make them more psychologically suited to the Party Plan concept.*

Venus:
The Party Plan Planet

You're likely familiar with John Gray's bestselling book, *Men Are from Mars, Women Are from Venus.* Early in the book, Gray makes this observation about the differences between the sexes:

> **A man's sense of self is defined through his ability to achieve results. A woman's sense of self is defined through her feelings and the quality of her relationships.**

There are, of course, exceptions to this observation, but for the most part, I'd say Gray hit the nail on the head as far as what makes women tick. Research shows that, across cultures, women are more in tune with their feelings and the feelings of others than men are, and women value and nurture their relationships more than men do. Which is what Party Plan marketing is all about — building solid, long-term relationships in a sharing, caring environment.

In the coming chapters, we'll talk about the psychology of success as it relates to recruiting and retention. But first, I need to lay the groundwork for those chapters by pointing out the key psychological attributes of women that distinguishes us from men... and why those attributes make women ideally suited for the Party Plan business concept.

Once you understand how we women are wired, then you'll have a richer perspective with which to analyze the psychology behind *your* behaviors, as well as the psychology driving the behaviors of the women you're seeking to recruit and retain. When all is said and done, your ability to GET women in your business — and, more importantly, your ability to KEEP them in the business — is directly correlated to your understanding of what makes women tick.

You're Wired to Multi-Task

Let's start by talking about the most important organ in the human body, the brain. To use a computer analogy, think of the brain as the software that runs the body. If men's brains are 1.0 version of cerebral software, then women are 1.4, for *women have four times more brain cells connecting the left and right side of the brain.* Whereas men rely mainly on the left brain (the analytical side) to solve problems, women access both sides, which enables women to solve multiple problems at one time and makes us better suited to

Think of the brain as the software that runs the body. If men's brains are 1.0 version of cerebral software, then women are 1.4, for women have four times more brain cells connecting the left and right side of the brain.

multi-tasking. (Now you know why we women can juggle kids, cooking, cleaning, and a full-time job).

Relationships Always on the Front Burner

When it comes to solving problems, men and women are both after the same end result. But because men are more goal oriented and because they focus so intently on the end **product**, sometimes the **process** may be less than diplomatic.

For women, on the other hand, **the PROCESS of problem solving is just as important as the end product.** Women view problems as an opportunity to deepen and strengthen relationships. A perfect example is shopping. When men need to shop for, say, a widget, they go straight to the widget department, compare features and prices of each widget, make their choice, and head to the shortest checkout line so that they can get on with their day.

> *For women, on the other hand, the PROCESS of problem solving is just as important as the end product. Women view problems as an opportunity to deepen and strengthen relationships.*

Women, on the other hand, call up a girlfriend or two and schedule an afternoon of widget shopping. On the way to the widget store, they may stop for lunch in the historic district and browse the window displays in the antique shops. If they come home empty handed, the shopping experience was still a success, for at the very least, the women spent a pleasant day with friends and got caught up on all the latest news.

Both sexes experienced the same event and had the same goal, but the process was very different. Women are usually concerned as much about *how* problems are solved as they are about the solution.

Women's Intuition

We've all heard the phrase, "women's intuition," and recent research indicates it's very real — and very useful — in helping women negotiate their lives. Webster defines intuition as *"the ability to perceive or know things without conscious reasoning."* There's such a thing as men's intuition also, but research indicates that men rely much more heavily on logic and reasoning to arrive at a solution. Men are more likely to break down problems into parts and deal with the parts in sequence.

> *Because women are inclined to see more interconnectedness, they're more likely to consider the subtleties than men.*

Women, on the other hand, tend to consider multiple sources of information and are more global in their perspective. Because women are inclined to see more interconnectedness, they're more likely to consider the subtleties than men. Little wonder, then, why we women talk three to four times more than men — talking (and listening to others' points of view) helps us kick our intuition into high gear.

Same Vacation, Different Memories

Because we women are more attuned to feelings, it's not surprising that men and women recall the same events very differently. Men tend to recall experiences associated with competition and physical activities and measurable events. Whereas, women are adept at recalling emotional experiences.

If called upon to remember past vacations, for example, men are more likely to recall how many miles they drove, the cost of the hotel room, and how many rounds of golf they played (and who won, of course). Women, on the other hand, are more likely to recall the serenity of walks on the beach and the contentment of reading a book without the kids interrupting every five minutes.

It's No Sin to Be Sensitive

At one time or another, most women can recall a man telling them they need to "stop being so sensitive all the time." He's right about one thing — there is physiological evidence that women have heightened sensitivities to their environment. But stop being so sensitive? Not on your life.

Sensitivity is a good thing, for it's the cornerstone upon which our relationships are built and maintained. Unlike men, who feel validated by physical challenges — such as sports, competition, and outdoor activities — women feel closer and validated through sharing of experiences, talking, and emotional bonding. And, as most women can testify, some men tend to find sharing feelings and intimacy uncomfortable.

Differences in Communication Styles

The only occasion in which men talk more than women is during task-oriented groups comprised of both men and women. In this situation, men talk much more than women, likely a result of the male tendency to solve problems, as well as some men's need to exert authority within the group.

Women ask more questions than men and are more likely to use polite words.

Not surprisingly, men interrupt women during conversations more than women interrupt men, and men make more unqualified statements of fact ("The

26

sooner we do this, the better"), as opposed to women, who use more qualifiers ("I guess," "I think," "I suppose"). In addition, women ask more questions than men and are more likely to use polite words ("please" and "thank you").

In informal settings, women like to talk about personal and private things (problems in life, challenges with the children) whereas men talk about sports and hobbies. Women frequently use non-verbal communication to bond with others (such as standing closer, touching, eye contact, and hand gestures), whereas men are more reserved non-verbally, especially in conversations with other men.

Women Are Psychologically Suited for Party Plans

To recap, women are born with certain skills that make us natural-born Party Plan marketers. We are biologically and culturally disposed to talk... share... nurture... help... support... protect... praise... and teach — all of which are qualities necessary for success in most businesses, but most especially, in the Party Plan business concept.

The Party Plan concept, with its informal, home-based setting and low-pressure, fun-first approach, is an ideal way for women of all ages and backgrounds to set their own hours and accomplish their own goals.

To recap, women are born with certain skills that make us natural-born Party Plan marketers.

The bottom line is there are differences between men and women, and it only makes sense for us women to capitalize on our God-given gifts, whether our work is in the home or in the marketplace. And research would indicate that women and the Party Plan concept fit like a hand in a custom-made glove.

Replace "Either/Or" Thinking with "Both/And" Thinking

As an experienced psychotherapist, I can tell you that the biggest frustration women struggle with is our tendency to neglect our own needs in order to attend to the needs of others. As one of my busiest coaching clients said to me, "I'm always putting myself last on my Needs List. I put my family before myself. I put my friends before myself. I put my team members before myself. **Then I squeeze my needs in wherever I can.**"

> *The biggest frustration women struggle with is our tendency to neglect our own needs in order to attend to the needs of others.*

Unfortunately, for most of us, putting ourselves last is the rule, not the exception. We women are people pleasers who focus on others. As a result, most women see the world as an **"either/or"** proposition:

"Either I put my family first, **or** I'm a failure."

"Either I stay at home full time, **or** I neglect my children."

A healthier alternative to the either/or mindset is the **"both/and"** proposition:

"I can be **both** a good mother, **and** have a career."

"I can **both** meet my needs, **and** attend to the needs of others."

Making this simple yet powerful psychological adjustment to your thinking could be the catalyst you need to dramatically alter the way you balance your roles in life.

We women may tell ourselves we're doing the right thing by sacrificing our needs for others, but in the end, sweeping our needs under the rug leads to resentment and hostility. By denying our needs, we just inflate our own problems, instead of solving others' problems.

Choose "Both/And"

Thankfully, you don't have to put your needs in the backseat anymore. You can put them in the driver's seat, right where they belong! Today, if you don't fit into the cookie-cutter mold that someone else has made for you, then you can just make your own cookie cutter.

If YOU want to be a full-time mother, then great, stay at home.

> *"Life isn't about finding yourself. Life is about creating yourself."*

If YOU want to be **both** a mother **and** have a career, then do both. After all, it's your life. It's your time. And it's your choice.

As the author Mary McCarthy observed, "Life isn't about finding yourself. Life is about *creating yourself.*" A big step toward self-fulfillment is having the courage to create the life you want to live by choosing to do the things YOU want to do, not the things OTHER PEOPLE want you to do.

The key is to choose what's best for you. Choose wisely, and you'll live **both** happily... **and** well.

Gratitude Recruiting

*You can get anything in life you want if you'll
just help enough other people get what they want.*

**Zig Ziglar
motivational speaker**

P op quiz time. What do all of the following
organizations with very different agendas have in
common with Party Plan companies?
The Girl Scouts. The U.S. Army. Fortune 500 com-
panies. Universities. The American Cancer Society.
Cheerleading squads. Fitness clubs. Churches. Credit
Unions. The state police. Residential real estate com-
panies. Garden clubs. Sororities. Big Brother and Big
Sisters of America. Hospitals and nursing homes.
Republicans and Democrats.
The answer: *They all recruit.*
Doesn't make any difference whether the organiza-
tions are designed for profit or charity... for recreation
or work... for the private sector or the government... for

personal gain or the common good, virtually all organizations grow by recruiting like-minded members.

Truth is, recruiting isn't an option — it's a necessity! Without a steady flow of new members, organizations can't survive. No matter what your business or enterprise, it's either recruit... or die.

> *Truth is, recruiting isn't an option — it's a necessity! Without a steady flow of new members, organizations can't survive.*

Gratitude Recruiting: The Gift That Keeps on Giving

The best way to explain how you should think about recruiting is to tell you about a retirement party I recently attended. A friend named Jane was retiring after more than 30 years in the business. She'd worked hard and invested well during her career, and she wanted to spend more time with her husband and grandchildren.

More than 400 people were packed into a swanky hotel ballroom, and as I looked around the room amid all the tears and cheers, it dawned on me that *this one person* was able to make a profound difference in hundreds, if not thousands, of people's lives through the Party Plan business concept.

As I looked around at all the smiling faces, I kept thinking what a wonderful gift Jane had given the women in the room when she recruited them into her business. Jane was *grateful* for the relationships and the freedom and the money she had received from the Party Plan concept, and she openly shared that gift with others by recruiting them into her business.

What Jane had practiced for 30 years... and what vaulted her to the top of her company... was a concept I call **Gratitude Recruiting.** Years ago Jane had received a gift — the opportunity to join a Party Plan company — and knowing how much the gift had enriched her life, she expressed an "attitude of gratitude" when she recruited. As a result, her organization grew and her business flourished.

Recruiting: What's in a Name?

Some people in the industry prefer to use the term "sponsoring" instead of "recruiting." That's fine by me. If your company prefers the term sponsoring, then sponsoring it is. But for the purposes of this book, I've chosen to use the term recruiting. As Shakespeare observed more than 400 years ago, "What's in a name? A rose by any other name smells just as sweet." And recruiting by any other name is still the best way to grow your business and grow your profits.

You'd think that Gratitude Recruiting would be the rule, rather than the exception, given all of the benefits of the business.

Whether it's called recruiting or sponsoring, some people (most especially new people) have a negative attitude toward the concept. You'd think that **Gratitude Recruiting** would be the rule in the industry, rather than the exception, given all of the benefits of the business.

Just look at all of the positives about the business: scheduling your work around your life, instead of your life around your work... having fun while making money... touching lives... sharing state-of-the-art products... setting your own goals... working at your own pace... owning your own business... taking advantage of your God-given gifts as a woman... and joining a 75-year old industry that is positioned to grow for decades into the future.

What's not to be grateful for?

But unfortunately, all too many women focus on the negatives of recruiting, instead of the positives. During my long association with numerous business leaders from coast to coast, I can tell you that there are A LOT more positives than negatives about this industry. Yet sadly, all too many women self-sabotage their success by focusing on the negatives. Below are a few of the most common negative stories that women tell themselves. Notice how each of these scripts focuses on the worst-case scenario:

> *The key to Gratitude Recruiting is to reframe your mental scripts to focus on positive outcomes. Instead of focusing on what won't work, focus on the benefits that attracted you to the business.*

"I don't want to intrude on people."

"I'm not very good at this."

"She's too busy to want to join me in the business."

"I know she'll say 'no,' and I hate being rejected."

The key to **Gratitude Recruiting** is to reframe your mental scripts to focus on positive outcomes. Instead of focusing on what won't work, focus on the benefits that attracted you to the business:

"She's so outgoing this opportunity would be perfect for her."

"A flexible schedule would allow her to homeschool her children."

"She's always dreamed of owning her own business."

Let's take a moment to examine the psychological reasons why you or your team members may have negative attitudes about recruiting. Then we'll look at ways to intervene in the cycle of negative self-talk and replace a negative attitude with an attitude of gratitude.

How We Talk to Ourselves

The biggest single emotion that detours people from expressing feelings of **Gratitude Recruiting** is fear — fear of rejection… fear of embarrassment… fear of failure. Fear is a powerful emotion that dominates many people's lives, making them cautious and keeping them from realizing their full potential.

If you have fears about recruiting, rest assured that you have lots of company! But once you understand the psychology of fear, then the fear is less menacing and less real. When confronted with knowledge, understanding, and positive self talk, fears shrivel up, allowing you to push these fears to the side and take positive action.

The first step in dealing effectively with fear is to peel back the layers and learn what is really lurking under that foreboding black cloak. Let's start with my favorite definition of fear:

Fear is writing scary stories to yourself and then telling others.

When you reframe fear in this light, all of a sudden you realize that fear is like the Boogeyman we were terrified of as children, just a figment of our imaginations, as opposed to a real, looming, tangible thing.

Fears are just scary stories that we script in our imagination and then validate by retelling them to ourselves and others. The way we script scary stories is personified once again by the movie *The Wizard of Oz*. Remember how Dorothy and her friends tremble with fear when they finally get an audience with the Wizard? Then, when the little dog Toto pulls back a curtain to reveal a timid old man manipulating some levers, each character realizes

> *Fear is writing scary stories to yourself and then telling others.*

that THEIR IMAGINED STORY is far scarier than the REALITY.

Likewise, people who FEAR RECRUITING tell themselves stories that are FAR SCARIER than the REALITY. The most common scary stories people working the business tell themselves revolve around these plots:

"I can't do this."

"I don't want to impose on my friends."

"My prospect is too _____ to do this." (Insert your own description in the blank, such as "too pretty,"... "too rich,"... "too sophisticated"... "too popular"... "too busy,"... "too successful,"... etc.

"I'll embarrass myself."

"I don't want to make money from my friends."

"No one would want to do this with me."

"I'm not any good at recruiting."

Each of these stories starts out starring YOU in a negative narrative about a future event that climaxes in failure. With this mindset, it's little wonder that people avoid recruiting.

Change Your Script, and You Change Your Life

Let me ask you a question: Do you think my friend Jane whom I told you about at the beginning of this chapter could have retired financially free surrounded by hundreds of dear friends if the stories she told herself about recruiting started out like the ones I just listed?

Not a chance.

> *"Courage isn't the absence of fear. Courage is taking action in the face of fear."*

You see, Jane understood intuitively that in order to become successful, she had to rewrite her stories so that they had a positive plot. That's not to say that Jane was fearless. Like everyone, Jane had fears. But she also knew that to get where she wanted to go in life, she had to face her fears.

As Mark Twain observed, "Courage isn't the absence of fear. Courage is taking action in the face of fear." So, Jane, like other successful women in Direct Sales, started replacing her scary scripts with cheerful scripts by feeding her imagination positive thoughts and scenarios, rather than negative ones.

How did she cancel the negative scripts? By reminding herself of the positive facts about the company, the products, and the opportunity. By complimenting herself on her good decision to join the business. And by rehearsing all of the reasons other women would be attracted to the business — the flexible hours... having fun and making money... doing good for others while doing well for yourself.

By feeding her mind a steady diet of positives, Jane began practicing **Gratitude Recruiting**. Before talking with a prospect, Jane reminded herself that she had a gift, and that gifts are for giving. If the prospect accepted Jane's gift of joining her in the business, that was terrific. If the prospect refused Jane's gift, that was terrific also. Jane learned not to take the refusal of her gift personally. Jane gave her gift freely and often, and, as a result, her business grew and prospered.

The Feelings Formula

Have you ever heard the expression, "Perception is reality"? Truer words were never spoken, especially when it comes to recruiting people into your business. If you perceive that no one would want to join you in your business, then that perception becomes your reality, and you'll be destined to lead an organization of one.

If, on the other hand, you perceive you have the best opportunity in the world and EVERYONE would want to hear about it, then you're destined to find positive people who are eager to join you in the business.

Negative perceptions beget negative stories which beget negative outcomes. Positive perceptions beget positive stories which beget positive outcomes. It's as simple as that.

In effect, our explanation to ourselves as to why prospects don't respond in ways we want them to is attached to our perceptions, and our perceptions dominate the direction of our stories. Negative perceptions beget negative stories which beget negative outcomes. Positive perceptions beget positive stories which beget positive outcomes. It's as simple as that.

So, the question is, how can negative or fearful people redefine their reality so that they have positive outcomes, instead of negative ones? The key to setting the table for positive outcomes is to understand how feelings are formed. Here is a simple formula that explains our feelings:

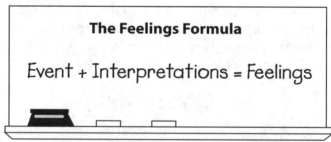

The Feelings Formula

Event + Interpretations = Feelings

Let's take a look at this formula in light of recruiting. Let's say you want to recruit an acquaintance who is a stay-at-home mom. You know she could use some extra income, but a nine-to-five job is out of the question, which makes her a perfect candidate for the business. She listens politely and then turns down the opportunity because she's, in her words, "too busy."

You tried to recruit her, but she turned you down. That was the EVENT.

But when you INTERPRETED that event in light of your scary story, it results in negative feelings, such as "I knew she wouldn't want to do this with me." Or, "I'm not very good at talking to people." Or, "I'm not meant to be in business for myself."

Now, here is where most people go wrong. When most people encounter negative feelings, *they try to control the EVENT, but what they need to control is their INTERPRETATION OF THE EVENT!* The key to becoming a successful recruiter, then, is to learn to intervene in the Feelings Formula and make the interpretation of the event positive, instead of negative. By making the psychological change from a negative spirit to a positive belief, you redefine your feelings about recruiting. In fact, by putting a positive spin on your interpretations of events, you can redefine your entire life, for the key to forging happy, loving relationships is learning to interpret everyday events in a positive, uplifting way.

> *When most people encounter negative feelings, they try to control the EVENT, but what they need to control is their INTERPRETATION OF THE EVENT!*

Folks, the Feelings Formula is a POWERFUL concept. Once you understand how feelings are created, you can consciously intervene in the process and turn a potentially negative feeling into a positive one. To better illustrate how you can head off negative interpretations and replace them with positive ones, I want you to imagine yourself in a scenario that I call the "Aunt Ethel Story."

The power of the Aunt Ethel story is that it forces people to reframe how they interpret their recruiting experiences so that they think of their prospects as being either **hungry** or **full**, instead of accepting or rejecting them. Remember this story from now on when you talk to prospects.

Aunt Ethel Story

Aunt Ethel invites you to join her for Thanksgiving dinner. You accept without hesitation because Aunt Ethel is your favorite aunt and the best cook in the whole world. Thanksgiving morning, you skip breakfast and lunch so you can eat more of Aunt Ethel's homemade dishes.

When dinner comes around, Aunt Ethel is at the top of her game. The turkey is tender and moist. The mashed potatoes are fluffy and buttered to perfection. And the corn bread stuffing is out of this world. You gobble up everything in sight. Just as you are pushing your chair back from your second giant serving, Aunt Ethel tiptoes to your side and cries out, *"Surprise! I saved the last slice of pumpkin pie just for you!"*

Sometimes people's lives are too full to accept the gift of joining you in the business.

You look up to see a beaming Aunt Ethel holding a thick slice of your favorite pumpkin pie. No one makes pumpkin pie like Aunt Ethel. You stare at the pie, watching the scoop of vanilla ice cream melt from the heat of the freshly-baked pie. But you're so full, you can't eat another bite, so you smile politely and raise your hands in surrender.

"Aunt Ethel, I love your pie, but I'm just too stuffed to eat so much as a single bite. I'm sorry, but at the moment, I'm just **too full**."

"Oh, that's okay, Dear," smiles Aunt Ethel. "I'll just wrap it up and you can take it with you."

The next day you open the refrigerator, and there is that slice of mouth-watering pumpkin pie. You're so **hungry** you can't stand it! You pour a big glass of milk, and you sit down to savor the pie that you've been thinking about for the last 24 hours. And much to your amazement, it's even better than you had imagined! You call Aunt Ethel and thank her for the pie, and everyone is as happy as a clam.

So remember, if they refuse your gift, they're not refusing YOU! At that moment, their lives are too full to accept your offer, so their refusal is about THEM, not you.

Applying the Feelings Formula to Recruiting

Now, let's look at the Aunt Ethel story in light of the **Feelings Formula: Event + Interpretation = Feelings.** During the **event** at Thanksgiving, you turned down Aunt Ethel's pumpkin pie. Aunt Ethel's **feelings** didn't get hurt because her **interpretation** of the event was positive instead of negative, right?

To become a successful recruiter, you have to adopt Aunt Ethel's attitude of gratitude. She gave the gift of the pie, but when you refused her gift, she didn't interpret it as a rejection. Instead, she understood that at that moment, you were **too full** to accept her gift.

You can influence your prospect's decision, but you can't make the decision for her.

Likewise, sometimes people's lives are **too full** to accept the gift of joining you in the business. Their lives may be *too full of kids.* Their lives may be *too full of problems.* Their lives may be *too full of work.* So remember, *if they refuse your gift, they're not* *refusing YOU!* At that moment, their lives are **too full** to accept your offer, so their refusal is about THEM, not you.

> *The key to effective recruiting is to take the responsibility for the decision OFF OF YOU and put it ONTO THE PROSPECT, where it belongs.*

Your Presentation, Their Decision

You can influence your prospect's decision, but you can't make the decision for her. Your job is to see if your prospects are **hungry,** but it's *their decision* as to whether they feel they're **too full** at the time to accept a slice of your opportunity.

If they're **too full** for your opportunity, do like Aunt Ethel — smile, and wrap up your opportunity for another day! Someday down the road, your friend may change her mind and be **hungry** for your opportunity.

The key to effective recruiting is to take the responsibility for the decision OFF OF YOU and put it ONTO THE PROSPECT, where it belongs. Remember, the opportunity is the gift, and you're the giver. If you give a gift and the prospect refuses it, that doesn't mean you should stop giving.

> *Remember, the opportunity is the gift, and you're the giver.*

Think of it this way. If you had a tradition of giving everyone you knew a present on Valentine's Day, and one of your friends returned your gift unopened, you wouldn't stop your tradition of gift giving, would you? I sure hope not!

Same goes for recruiting. Just because a prospect is **too full** at that moment to join you in your business is no reason to stop offering the gift to others who might need it and appreciate it.

With Gratitude Recruiting, you're sure to get more people to join you in your business. Once your recruiting improves, the $64,000-dollar question becomes, "How do I keep my recruits from dropping out of the business?"

To discover the answer to that question, let's turn to the next chapter, titled, *Retention: The Elephant in the Living Room.*

CHAPTER FOUR

Retention:
The Elephant in the Living Room

You don't drown by falling in the water.
You drown by staying there.

Katherine Hepburn

Y ou don't have to be married long to know the full meaning of the expression, "The honeymoon is over." The expression, of course, doesn't mean the marriage is over. Just means that **reality** has kicked **romance** out of the driver's seat. For committed couples, when the honeymoon is over, it means it's time to cancel the cruise control and start steering the relationship through the emotional roadblocks that threaten to wreck the marriage.

Like marriage, your business has a honeymoon period, too. According to research, the honeymoon in Direct Sales ends somewhere around eight weeks in the business, when **romance** ("I love this product...," "I love this opportunity...," "I love my sponsor...," etc.) gives way to **reality** ("I'm just not cut out for this...," "No one returns my phone calls...," "I'm not good at sales," etc.).

Yes, the honeymoon period in Direct Sales is destined to end. But just as every newly-wedded couple doesn't end up in divorce court, every new recruit doesn't end up dropping out of the business. The key to retention in your business is the same as it is in marriage — success is a matter of awareness of the realities and challenges facing you, combined with a willingness to learn and implement strategies that will bring about the outcomes you and your partners want.

Like marriage, your business has a honeymoon period, too. According to research, the honeymoon in Direct Sales ends somewhere around eight weeks in the business.

Retention: The Elephant in the Living Room

Abraham Lincoln once remarked, "You cannot escape the reality of tomorrow by evading it today." Honest Abe understood that ignoring impending problems doesn't make them go away. The only way to solve a problem is to acknowledge it and take action to solve it.

"You cannot escape the reality of tomorrow by evading it today."

Hands down, the biggest challenge you'll face in your business is **retention**. It's the elephant in the living room that everyone tiptoes around but no one wants to talk about. Well, you have to deal with that elephant, or it's going to stampede and destroy your house.

Have you ever wondered why so many women enter the business excited and fired up, only to drop out after a few weeks or months? Most companies and leaders assume that the key to better retention is to provide support by way of GOOD training... GOOD products... and GOOD mentoring. Yes, those GOOD things help new recruits. That is, the GOOD stuff helps new recruits until something BAD happens to them, and then, *bam!* — they drop out of the business.

Why? Because most leaders are so focused on keeping things positive that they don't talk about the realities that everyone in the business must face. As a result, people new to the business aren't psychologically prepared for the BAD things they'll inevitably have to deal with — that is, the disappointments... the rejections... the no-shows, etc.

Hands down, the biggest challenge you'll face in your business is retention. It's the elephant in the living room that everyone tiptoes around but no one wants to talk about.

Reality Check: Bad Things Happen to Even the Best People

Yes, you have to focus on the positives in the business, that goes without saying. But you also have to recognize that negative experiences are inevitable in this business (just as they are in life). Because humans are more motivated to *avoid pain* than to seek pleasure, most new people drop out of the business when the honeymoon is over. Since the honeymoon period has to end sooner or later, doesn't it make sense to prepare your people for the bad times, as well as the good ones?

That's what this chapter is about. In the coming pages, you'll learn about the three most common negative feelings that people in the business experience, and you'll learn proven strategies to help you and your new recruits effectively manage the emotional issues that pop up repeatedly in this business.

The key to improving retention rates starts with self awareness, and the first thing to be aware of is that EVERYONE will hit the reality rapids in this business. Successful people ride the rapids and stay on board, knowing that calmer waters lie ahead. Dropouts, on the other hand, jump overboard and swim for the shore when the ride starts to get rocky. By understanding the psychology that provokes people to drop out, you can intervene and throw your recruits a life line when you see them floundering and struggling to stay afloat.

> *Yes, you have to focus on the positives in the business, that goes without saying. But you also have to recognize that negative experiences are inevitable in this business (just as they are in life).*

Life Happens

The number one problem that everyone faces in this business can be summed up in two words: **Life happens.** John Lennon, the major creative force behind the Beatles, put it this way: *"Life is what happens while you're making other plans."*

Boy, is that the truth! You plan on working the business, and then — BAM! — *life happens!* Your parents get sick. Or your teenage son wrecks the car. Or your husband loses his job. Or you run headlong into a midlife crisis. Or a hostess cancels on you at the last minute because her grandmother died. Or you get five refusals in a row. When life happens, your emotions start ricocheting around like

> *The number one problem that everyone faces in this business can be summed up in two words: Life happens.*

a pin ball, and you start doubting yourself: "Why am I doing this business?"

So, what do most people in the business do when the honeymoon is over and reality sets in? All too often, they quit. Folks, it doesn't have to happen this way! No, you can't change certain realities. But you can change how *you respond* to those realities — and you can *teach others* how to respond more positively to the realities in their lives... and they can teach others, with the net effect of more people having fun and making money, and, as a result, higher retention.

> No, you can't change certain realities. But you can change how you respond to those realities.

Think about it — wouldn't it be great if the dropout rate could be significantly reduced? Wouldn't that make your business more fun and more profitable? Well, once you and your team understand the psychological factors that cause people to throw in the towel, then you can teach others the coping strategies that will empower them to deal with the emotional issues that EVERY-ONE in this industry will face.

You're in the Emotional Relationship Business

When a reporter asked Howard Schultz, the founder of Starbucks, how the coffee business was doing, he replied, *"Don't know. Our business isn't about coffee. Our business is about relationships."*

Like Schultz, successful business builders understand that their business isn't JUST ABOUT the product or the opportunity, but their business is ALL ABOUT **emotional relationships.**

In my seminars, I emphasize this is an emotional business. People **buy in** the business on an emotional high, and they **buy out** of the business on an emotional low. What the dropouts fail to realize is that EVERY-ONE in the business feels negative emotions from time to time. Successful people aren't immune to negative feelings. They've just learned to manage their feelings, rather than let their feelings manage them. So, when successful people hit a low, they don't drop out. They persevere in the face of adversity, recognizing that low periods don't last forever.

> *Successful people aren't immune to negative feelings. They've just learned to manage their feelings, rather than let their feelings manage them.*

The three most common negative feelings you and your people will experience are **disappointment, anger,** and **depression.** Let's take a closer look at each of these feelings to learn what causes them and how they can undermine your success.

1) **Disappointment:** The root cause of disappointment originates with unrealistic expectations of ourselves and others. When you EXPECT others to always behave in a way that benefits you, then you're just setting yourself up for disappointment. Unrealistic self-talk, such as "**They should** return my phone calls" or "**They should** work as hard as I do," just invite disappointment. Disappointment is something you do to yourself. When you say things like, "**I should** be further along in the business" or "**I should** be making more money," you're measuring yourself against an expectation. Instead, **measure yourself by your actions, not your results.** Do the right thing enough times, and the results will come.

2) **Anger:** Everybody in this business gets frustrated from time to time. Maybe you get tired of hearing "no." Maybe your husband isn't as supportive as you'd like. You can try to analyze or contain your anger, but that doesn't defuse it. The best way to deal with anger is to **protest it** (getting your anger out). Take five minutes and stomp around a bit. Pound a pillow or vent to a friend. Get your anger OUT, for anger turned inward becomes depression. One exercise I teach to help people get their anger out is to have them imagine firing all of the people who won't follow directions. Give yourself permission in your fantasy to fire the people who frustrate you by pointing at them like Donald Trump in *The Apprentice* and shouting, "You're fired!" This exercise will get your energy back and move you through obsessing.

3) **Depression:** Here's an alarming statistic: 87% of women are depressed at some time in their lives. Most depression is **situational depression**. An event in our lives sends us into a temporary tailspin. Depression is characterized by lack of energy. No excitement. No focus. No passion in life. Chronic sadness. And sleep problems. **Situational depression** can be resolved by protesting it, exercising, or talking with a therapist or coach. People with long-term depression, six months or more, need to be evaluated by a physician.

"The Only Way Out, Is Through"

As we learned in the previous chapter, feelings are a combination of an **event** and the **interpretation of the event**. The interpretation part of the formula is where people get thrown off course. When someone doesn't return your phone calls, your **interpretation** may be that they're rude, which leads you to *feel* disappointed and angry. But the REALITY may be something entirely different. The person may be on vacation, in which case you've had to deal with a negative feeling of your own creation.

Even though our interpretations of events sometimes create inappropriate feelings, it doesn't mean those feelings are any less real. Whether you touch a hot stove accidentally or on purpose, you'll still get burned, and you'll still feel the pain of that burn, accident or no accident. Same with feelings. If you exaggerate a feeling or talk yourself into a feeling, you're still experiencing it, even if it's a creation of your imagination. The interpretation may have been off base, but the feeling is still real.

Psychotherapists have a saying about feelings: "The only way out, is through." In other words, you have to go through your feelings to be done with them.

That's why I tell my clients that **feelings are facts.** Like facts, feelings are real. Feelings are valid. You can't ignore your feelings, and you can't make them go away by sweeping them under the rug. Feelings can go in only two directions — IN... or OUT. When your feelings go IN, they don't get resolved. Like a furnace, feelings have to get vented, or they'll eventually explode from the built-up pressure.

Psychotherapists have a saying about feelings: *"The only way out, is through."* In other words, you have to go through your feelings to be done with them. You have to recognize your feelings... understand them... talk about them... and protest them if you want to put them behind you.

Getting rid of a negative feeling is a three-step process:

1) **Feel it**
2) **Express it**
3) **Release it**

Unfortunately, women have a tendency to *blame themselves* for their negative feelings by replaying negative self-talk that portrays them as inadequate... or incompetent... or unworthy... or not smart enough... or too disorganized... or whatever. (With that kind of self talk, no wonder so many women are depressed.)

> *Getting rid of a negative feeling is a three-step process:*
> *1) Feel it*
> *2) Express it*
> *3) Release it*

Keys to Retention:
Self Awareness and Intervention

Are you beginning to see how negative self-talk can motivate women to drop out of the business prematurely? If women blame themselves instead of outside forces for everything that goes wrong, then when things don't go as planned, many women will interpret the setbacks as evidence that they're failures or not up to the job. So they drop out, adding even more fuel to the fire of negative self-talk.

It's been my experience that most women who drop out would stay in the business longer if they understood the **Cycles of Change** that occur in every business, as well in everyone's personal lives. You see, most peo-

> *You see, most people operate under the misconception that life is linear, that life runs along a straight chronological line, and with each event, life just gets better and better.*

ple operate under the misconception that **life is linear,** that life runs along a straight chronological line, and with each event, life just gets better and better. First, you go to school. Then you graduate. Then you get a job. Then you get married. Then you have kids. Then you retire.

One problem with the life-is-linear theory. *It's a myth!*

> **One problem with the life-is-linear theory. It's a myth!**

I don't know of a single person whose life has progressed linearly. But I do know lots of people who have arrived at a great place in their lives by overcoming the adversities life has tossed in their paths.

In the next chapter, we'll take a closer look at the four **Cycles of Change** everyone goes through repeatedly in their lives. Once you learn to recognize and expect the Cycles of Change, then you'll be better equipped to keep your life and your business on an even keel. Best of all, by teaching your people to recognize and manage the **Cycles of Change**, you'll see your **retention rate soar** like never before!

...

Cycles of Change

For all your days prepare,
And meet them ever alike;
When you are the anvil, bear —
And when you are the hammer, strike.

Edwin Markham

The legendary advice columnist, Ann Landers, was once asked what would be her one single most useful piece of advice for all of humanity. Without a hesitation, Landers replied:

"My advice to everyone is to expect trouble as an inevitable part of life, and when it comes, hold your head high, look it squarely in the eye and say, 'I will be bigger than you. You cannot defeat me.' Then repeat to yourself the most comforting of all words, 'This too shall pass.'"

When Ann Landers says "... to expect trouble as an inevitable part of life," what she's referring to are the **Cycles of Change**. Life is a circular process, like riding a Ferris Wheel through time. We get on at the bottom of the cycle, and we ride it up and down, high and low, from birth until death. The people who thrive in life and in business live by Landers' advice to repeat this refrain: "This too shall pass."

Message of the Maples

Ever notice how some people whine and complain about every ache and pain and mishap, while others with much more serious ailments and problems remain cheerful and upbeat?

What accounts for the difference in how people handle adversity?

Choice.

Some of us choose to be **victims.** Others choose to be **victors.** In the end, it's **choice,** not **chance,** that determines our destiny.

There's a classic story called the *Message of the Maples* that illustrates the importance of remaining strong and positive in the face of adversity. The story was written by Edgar Jackson and was inspired by his real-life struggle to regain his speech after suffering a stroke.

> *Some of us choose to be victims. Others choose to be victors. In the end, it's choice, not chance, that determines our destiny.*

After months of rehab, Jackson learned to talk again. He moved to a farm in Vermont to write and reflect. One day a neighbor was complaining to Jackson about a long list of personal problems. After listening patiently, Jackson invited the neighbor for a walk. They arrived at a three-acre pasture encircled by maple trees and a barbed wire fence. Jackson explained that instead of setting fence posts, the previous owner had planted the maple trees and then ran barbed wire from one tree to the next.

Jackson walked from tree to tree with the neighbor, pointing out how each tree responded to the barbed wire wrapped around its trunk. Some of the trees had incorporated the barbed wire into their trunks and were growing strong and upright. But some of the trees never adjusted to the barbs, and they grew twisted and deformed.

Jackson explained that people are like these maple trees. Some people encounter setbacks and challenges in their lives and adjust to them by incorporating them in their lives. These people grow tall and triumphant despite their hardships. Other people allow their challenges to twist and distort their lives.

"The difference between trees and people," Jackson said to the neighbor, "is that trees can't choose how they will grow. People can."

Four Cycles of Change

Message of the Maples could just as easily be titled, Message of the Business, for, like the trees in Jackson's pasture, you're going to have to deal with some barbs in your business. Your business won't progress linearly upward, like a straight line on a graph. Your business will go through the four **Cycles of Change,** and when it spins into a low point, you're faced with a choice. Do you become a victor by remaining straight and strong? Or do you become a victim, allowing the barbs to weaken your resolve and deform your dreams?

> *Your business won't progress linearly upward, like a straight line on a graph. Your business will go through the four Cycles of Change.*

Landers and Jackson were victors because they understood that life moves through cycles, and when life hit a low point in the cycle, they dealt with it until it passed.

Cycles of Change will occur in your business, as

well as in your life. There are four main **Cycles of Change** that you'll go through again and again in your business. Once you learn to recognize and understand these **Cycles of Change**, you'll be better able to manage your emotions and keep yourself on an even keel during the ups... and the downs.

The four **Cycles of Change** are as follows:

1) **Go for It**
2) **The Doldrums**
3) **Cocooning**
4) **Getting Ready**

Let's describe each of these stages in more detail so that you can identify where you are right now in your business. Then we'll look at some strategies for keeping your emotions in equilibrium during the times you're highest and lowest in the cycle.

1) **Go for It:** This is the high point of the cycle. Self talk is characterized by thoughts like, "I'm doing the work I want to do. It's fabulous. I'm loving it, having fun and making money. I'm achieving my goals, feeling good about myself and the choice I made." During the Go for It phase, you feel confident. In control. Fulfilled. Then something unexpected happens, like an illness. Or a falling out with a friend. Or a key person in your organization drops out. As a result, negative emotions flare up as you move into a lower cycle.

2) **The Doldrums:** This period in the life cycle is like a little death. This phase is characterized by self-doubt. You feel out of sync. You're stuck in a low point, you're pessimistic, and you can't see the way out. You may feel slightly depressed, perhaps even deeply depressed. You lack energy

and direction. You can't motivate yourself to pick up the phone to make the next call because you dread the outcome.

3) **Cocooning:** During this stage of the life cycle, you become more introspective. You go inward, asking questions, seeking answers to your roles in life, questioning your values, searching for a new identity. You start to reassess your passion and purpose with probing questions like, "Who am I? Am I doing the work I want?" This phase leads to feelings of rebirth and self-renewal, which gradually evolves into the final stage of the cycle.

4) **Getting Ready:** In this phase, you're moving from *inward* questioning to *outward* action. You start experimenting by doing things you've been putting off or trying new activities. You take classes, ask questions, read books, enroll in seminars, and start dreaming again. You start to reformulate the vision you have for your life, and the knowledge and self confidence you've gained encourages you to become even bolder, until, BAM!, you're right back in the "Go for It" stage of the life cycle.

If you look back on your adult life, you'll recognize that you've gone through the four phases of the life cycle many times before. In my own life, I've had periods in the life cycle that lasted for months. When my brother died in 1999, for example, I spent a year in **The Doldrums,** deeply depressed, with no apparent end in sight.

But I let the life cycle take its natural course, and eventually, I moved to the **Cocooning** period, where I questioned the meaning of life and my place in it, to the **Getting Ready** phase, where I started getting excited about work again and regained my passion and purpose. Right now I'm in the **Go for It** phase, fired up about what I'm doing and excited about working with my long-standing clients and eagerly working on several new projects. Life is great!

To become a **victor,** rather than a **victim,** in your life and in business, it helps to understand that life progresses in a series of cycles, not in a linear straight line. Victors in life and in the business **expect lows** along with the highs. They don't throw in the towel during lows. They just hang in there and do what they can to make the cycle head upward again.

Key to Success

The key to managing the **Cycles of Change** is fourfold:

First, *accept the Cycles of Change.* Acceptance means giving yourself permission not to feel bad or inadequate when you hit a low point. Low points are to be expected. When you hit The Doldrums, it doesn't mean there's something wrong with you. Like it or not, you're going to go through low cycles because the four **Cycles of Change** are as natural as the four seasons. When winter arrives, you don't blame yourself, do you? Of course not. To survive winter, you make the best of it, knowing that spring is right around the corner. Same goes for the seasons of the business.

Acceptance means giving yourself permission not to feel bad or inadequate when you hit a low point.

Second, *teach yourself and your people to recognize the Cycles of Change.* Self knowledge is crucial to shaping healthy lives and businesses, and people who are aware of where they are in the cycle of change will be better equipped to work their way through every position of the Ferris Wheel of life.

Third, *know which phase you and your people are in.* That way you can give your teammates the encouragement and support to keep working the business while they weather the low periods. The longer you let bad things drain your energy, the longer you postpone your dream. The problem with staying in The Doldrums is that bad thoughts, like mushrooms, grow in the dark. You WILL experience The Doldrums, but you don't want to resign yourself to dwelling there.

> *The longer you let bad things drain your energy, the longer you postpone your dream. The problem with staying in The Doldrums is that bad thoughts, like mushrooms, grow in the dark.*

Fourth, *learn and teach your people the strategies to deal with these cycles.* To weather the low cycles and reach your full potential, you have to learn and teach your people the **Feelings Formula**... learn and teach your people the principles of **Gratitude Recruiting**... learn and teach your people that "the only way out is through," and so on. The strategies in this book are designed to move people through The Doldrums so that you can start making money and having fun again.

Once you learn to recognize where you are in the **Cycles of Change** in your life and your business... and once you teach your people to recognize the phases they're in... then you'll be in a position to manage your feelings and get back on the road to having fun and making money.

CHAPTER SIX

Stopping Self-Sabotage!

We have met the enemy, and he is us.

Walt Kelly
cartoonist of Pogo

Self-Sabotage.

It's what dooms the major characters in Shakespeare's tragedies.

It's what provides the tabloids with an endless stream of celebrity scandals.

And, on a more personal note, it's what derails us from our dreams, for Self-Sabotage turns good people into their own worst enemies. As a former client of mine put it, *"I always figure out a way to snatch defeat from the jaws of victory."*

Self-Sabotage. We recognize it in our friends and loved ones:

The pretty ex-sorority sister who keeps falling for married men.

The brilliant brother who can't keep a job.

The excited new recruit who sells hundreds of dollars of products right out of the gate and then suddenly quits.

The team member who's on her way to becoming a leader and then freezes and can't remember how to meet her goals.

Yes, we see Self-Sabotage at work in the people around us, and we shake our heads in dismay. But, ironically, we have a hard time seeing self-sabotage in ourselves!

Understanding Self-Sabotage

Self-Sabotage. We all do it. Famous or unknown. Rich or poor. Male or female. To a greater or lesser degree, we all act out an unconscious script that directs us to sabotage our hopes and dreams.

When I was working as a psychotherapist, I used to counsel people who wanted more in their lives. I noticed that some people never seemed to get what they wanted. At first I tried to shrug it off by saying they hadn't really committed themselves to therapy or that they weren't working hard enough for their goals. But many of my clients worked *really hard,* but *still* they weren't able to achieve what they wanted in their lives.

"If you think you can... or you think you can't... you're right." Negative belief systems become self-fulfilling prophesies that keep women unconsciously tied to a short leash.

I began to ask myself, "With all their genuine motivation and the application of the techniques they learned in therapy, *WHY* didn't they improve?"

The answer is *they didn't believe they DESERVED* to get what they said they wanted. So, like Sisyphus in Greek mythology, they pushed a boulder up the hill every day to reach their wants, only to trip over their own feet and watch helplessly as the boulder tumbled to the bottom of the hill.

Main Reasons People Self-Sabotage

There are two main reasons people Self-Sabotage. One, they have a **negative belief system.** They repeat negative scripts about themselves that undermine their dreams. Two common self-sabotaging scripts I hear women in this business rehearse are, "I can't be a leader because I'll have to deal with too many people;" or, "I can't be a success because I'll have to give up my family." As Henry Ford observed, "If you think you can... or you think you can't... you're right." Negative belief systems become self-fulfilling prophesies that keep women unconsciously tied to a short leash.

We "inherit" our permissions from the myths, statements, reprimands, and criticisms we hear from our families and important mentors.

The second main reason for Self-Sabotage is **lack of permission from your past.** Each of us is programmed by our upbringing and experiences. We "inherit" our permissions from the myths, statements, reprimands, and criticisms we hear from our families and important mentors. Thus, as an adult, our personal beliefs about ourselves are deeply embedded in our permission system. Most of these permissions were encoded into our unconscious before the age of five. Unless we consciously update our permissions, they will inform and direct our thoughts and decisions throughout our lives.

For example, several years ago I met a bright, energetic woman who had a tremendous fear of recruiting. She was outgoing and a natural leader, but she dreaded the thought of sharing the business with others. As we talked about her past, I learned that when she was eight years old, she came home excited about selling girl scout cookies. Her father burst her bubble of enthusiasm, telling her he wouldn't let her "sell these cookies because I don't want you to bother the neighbors." Fast forward 30 years. The woman was trying to build a business, but she couldn't pick up the phone because her dad's words, "Don't bother the neighbors," kept coming back to haunt her.

Unfortunately, because most people don't update their permission scripts in adulthood, they spend their lives living out the permission scripts they learned as children.

Unfortunately, because most people don't update their **permission scripts** in adulthood, they spend their lives living out the permission scripts they learned as children. When these negative scripts from the past are applied to the present, they prevent people from building a business.

Fear: The Fatal Attraction

The permissions from the past that have the strongest hold on us are the ones borne out of our fears, for, as a famous psychologist wrote, *"Whatever we fear has already happened to us."* Problem is, **our past predicts our future.**

For instance, if we were abandoned as children, we will fear abandonment as adults. So, fearing more abandonment, we will "protect" ourselves by abandoning someone before they abandon us.

If we fear rejection from a prospect, we'll reject ourselves first by not approaching that person and then rationalizing it by blaming them: "They won't be interested, so why bother?"

If we fear intimacy, we'll date (or even marry) people we can never get close to.

If we fear success, we'll make sure we never get it. (Or, if we finally attain success, we'll make sure we do something to sabotage it).

It's our unconscious memories of fear and pain that make us so prone to Self-Sabotage. Paradoxically, by focusing on our fears and past pains, we increase the likelihood of experiencing them again.

> *The vast majority of our fears are imagined, no more real than the boogeyman hiding in our childhood closet. According to research, 98% of our fears are unreal.*

If all of our fears were real, it would be easy to understand why people would be eager to dance to their tune. But the vast majority of our fears are imagined, no more real than the boogeyman hiding in our childhood closet. According to research, 98% of our fears are unreal.

But because energy and action follow our thoughts, the more we think and obsess about our fears, the more we make them real. One wit aptly described the crippling effect of fear this way: *"Fear is that little dark room where negatives are developed."*

> *"Fear is that little dark room where negatives are developed."*

By constantly worrying and replaying negative scripts, we plant and nurture the fears that will grow into vines that strangle our dreams.

Self Awareness: The Antidote to Self-Sabotage

Fortunately, we don't have to fall victim to the subconscious voices that undermine our success. The first step to breaking the cycle of Self-Sabotage is to "know yourself." Not just your conscious self, but your unconscious self, for without self-knowledge, you're destined to repeat the patterns of failure.

Self-Sabotage is an emotional straight jacket that constrains our behaviors and feelings, binding us tightly with negative subconscious straps that keep us from reaching out and grabbing what we want most in life.

But self-awareness unbuckles the bindings, and positive self-talk frees your arms to grab and hold onto the things you want most in life. The key to mastering fear and stopping Self-Sabotage is twofold.

First, you need to raise your **Deserve Level**. And second, you need to replace the self-defeating **Sabotage Strategies** with positive self-talk and self-nurturing.

How We Define Our Deserve Levels

Your **Deserve Level** is comprised of your conscious and unconscious beliefs about what you *can* and *are supposed* to achieve in life.

Your Deserve Level is comprised of your conscious and unconscious beliefs about what you can and are supposed to achieve in life.

Just as your IQ indicates the boundaries to your intelligence, your **Deserve Level** indicates the boundaries to what you *think* you deserve in life. The good news is that unlike IQ levels, **Deserve Levels** are self-chosen and can be raised.

Your final verdict on what you deserve is based on your conscious and unconscious feelings and beliefs. There are specific **Deserve Levels** for every area of our lives: Love... work... friends... health... happiness... income, etc.

Because each of these areas is separate, it's possible to have a high **Deserve Level** in one area (career) and a low **Deserve Level** in a different area (relationships). Which would explain why Elizabeth Taylor could earn millions as a successful movie star yet have seven failed marriages.

We all start out in life with the potential for a high **Deserve Level**. As babies, we feel we deserve to be held and fed and fussed over. We scream when we're hungry or wet, and we throw tantrums when we don't get our way. And we don't feel any need to apologize or justify our behavior. Then, over time, our innate sense of feeling that we deserve love just for "being" gives way to our attempts to earn love by "doing."

> *What we eventually define as our Deserve Level in adulthood will profoundly affect what we get out of life, for, in the end, we get what we believe we deserve. No more, no less.*

As we get older, through our experiences and our INTERPRETATIONS of those experiences, we begin defining ourselves and our place in the world, laying the foundation for our adult **Deserve Level**.

How Your Deserve Level Impacts Your Life and Your Business

What we eventually define as our **Deserve Level** in adulthood will profoundly affect what we get out of life, for, in the end, **we get what we believe we deserve.** No more, no less. **We never exceed our own expectations, at least not for long.** If we do happen to exceed our expectations, our unconscious will release **Self-Sabotage Strategies** that will chase us back into the boundaries of our **Deserve Level**.

The challenge of Self-Sabotage is that if we achieve beyond our comfort zone, we face a choice. We can either increase our **Deserve Level** limits to accommodate our achievements, or we can give away what we have achieved. Sadly, many people choose to give away their achievements.

Increasing Your Deserve Level

Just as each of us has a "metabolic set point" that controls our weight, we also have a "psychological set point" that determines our **Deserve Level**. The good news is that just as your metabolic set point can be adjusted through diet and exercise, your psychological set point can be altered by awareness and a willingness to change.

In everyone's life, there is a gap between what we *want* and what we *believe* we deserve. **The bridge between that gap is our expectations.**

People with low **Deserve Levels** and low self-esteem and low self-confidence will build that bridge with **negative expectations:** "I don't deserve it, so *I'll sabotage* getting it."

People with high **Deserve Levels** and high self-esteem and high self-confidence will build that bridge with **positive expectations:** "I deserve it, and *I'll facilitate* getting it."

Take a moment to analyze your **Deserve Level** by answering the following five questions openly and honestly. The first part of the five questions indicates a *low* **Deserve Level**. The second part indicates a *high* **Deserve Level**.

1) Do you refuse to dream so that you won't be disappointed with your present life?... Or do you have lofty dreams and desires?

2) Do you only recruit prospects less qualified than you?... Or do you seek out people who are community leaders or have successful careers?

3) Do you take the road of least resistance most of the time?... Or do you stretch and challenge yourself?

4) Do you find yourself making excuses for why you don't have more and aren't doing more in your life?... Or are you taking actions RIGHT NOW to make your future happier and more prosperous?

5) Do you learn from your past mistakes and move on to make wiser decisions?... Or do you keep repeating the same mistakes over and over again?

If you have a low **Deserve Level**, you can make a conscious effort to raise it by breaking out of your comfort zone and dreaming bigger dreams. If you have a high **Deserve Level** and you're still falling far short of your expectations, you may be unconsciously undermining your dreams by practicing common **Self-Sabotage Strategies.**

Let's take a moment to look at the five most common **Self-Sabotage Strategies** that people use to make sure they stay well within their **Deserve Level**.

Self-Sabotage Strategies

Every day of the week, intelligent, motivated people self-sabotage their dreams by resorting to unconscious strategies that prevent them from reaching or holding onto their desired outcome.

Following are the five most common **Self-Sabotage Strategies** that keep people within their self-chosen limits. Notice the negative self-talk that accompanies each of these self-defeating strategies:

Five Common Self-Sabotage Strategies

1) **Throwing It Away:** "I achieve my dream or goal, and then, because I don't truly believe I deserve it, I blow it."

2) **Denial:** "I know I have a problem that's holding me back, but facing it is painful. So, if I ignore it, maybe it will go away."

3) **The Fatal Flaw:** "I'm aware that I have a BIG PERSONALITY PROBLEM that undoes all of my best efforts (excessive drinking, out-of-control gambling, addiction to drugs, hair-trigger temper, perfectionism, criticism of self and others, arrogance, poor listener, refusal to grow, intolerance, etc.), but I refuse to face my flaw and change my behavior."

4) **Resignation:** "Deep down, I don't believe I deserve (a successful career... the man of my dreams... more money... happiness, etc.), so I won't even start down that path, or I'll stop myself before I get there."

5) **Settling:** "I want it, but I don't believe I'm good enough, so I'll settle for less. I probably won't get what I want anyway, so I won't try very hard. That way I won't be as disappointed when I fail."

The common thread running through all of these **Self-Sabotage Strategies** is the underlying sense that you don't deserve the desired goal. In other words, you don't *believe* you're worthy of achieving the things you desire. So, you obey your belief system by staying safely within your **Deserve Level** or by giving back any achievements that exceed your **Deserve Level**.

Sad what our unconscious does to hold us back, isn't it? And hold us back, it will, unless we go to the core of the issue and start changing self-limiting beliefs into empowering beliefs.

Life Beliefs:
The Inner Voice That Directs Our Lives

If you've ever seen or participated in a square dance, then you know that the dance steps are dictated by the "caller." While the music plays, the caller shouts out the steps, and the dancers change partners and make moves based on the caller's instructions.

Well, our conscious and unconscious Belief System is like the caller at a square dance. As we dance through life, our LIFE BELIEFS tell us what moves we need to make in response to each new experience.

Our conscious and unconscious Belief System is like the caller at a square dance. As we dance through life, our LIFE BELIEFS tell us what moves we need to make in response to each new experience.

Our beliefs are the repetitive statements that we make to and about ourselves. Our beliefs are reflected in the people we choose to love, the friends we cultivate, the music we listen to, the careers we pursue, the amount of money we earn, and so on. We hold our beliefs so dearly that we consider them as facts. (They must be true and factual or we wouldn't believe them, right?). So, it's our *old beliefs* that dictate how we respond to *new experiences.*

We all have beliefs. Nothing wrong with that. Without beliefs, we'd be rudderless. Positive beliefs keep us on the straight and narrow, reminding us to do the right thing in the face of temptations.

But, unfortunately, we also have negative beliefs which we also accept as true and factual. If we're taught by our parents that "You'll never amount to anything," or taught by your peers that "You're not cute enough to run with the popular crowd," then we internalize those criticisms, rehearse them, and then file them away as facts.

The Power of Beliefs

Why do beliefs exercise so much power over our lives? Two reasons. One, *energy follows thought;* and two, *whatever you think about, expands.* Let's take a moment to examine how each of these two manifestations of our beliefs shape our lives.

> *Why do beliefs exercise so much power over our lives? Two reasons. One, energy follows thought; and two, whatever you think about, expands.*

Energy Follows Thoughts: Have you ever had those days when nothing goes right? Your children keep interrupting you while you're trying to make recruiting calls. You return from lunch with a prospect only to discover that you've left your cell phone at the restaurant. You jump in your car to retrieve your cell phone and the car has a flat tire.

Mercifully, your workday finally comes to an end. You're tired and depressed. All you want to do is crawl in bed and pull the covers over your head.

The phone rings. It's someone you've been trying to recruit for two months. She's calling to tell you she's been laid off. Previously, she'd been **too full** to join you in your business, but now that her circumstances have changed, she's **hungry** for your opportunity. She wants to know if she can get together with you tonight to sign up and get started!

Suddenly, your energy level surges, doesn't it? Why? Because as your thoughts change from gloomy to glad, your energy level switches from sluggish to fired up.

Whatever You Think About, Expands: What you focus on is what you get more of. If your prospect had not called, you likely would have stayed tired and depressed all evening. You would have gone to bed tired and depressed. And likely woken up tired and depressed.

But once your prospect called, your spirits soared. Your depression melted away. Your energy was restored. Now that your thoughts were focused on signing up a new prospect, your **positive thoughts expanded** into all areas of your life.

Are You Asking for too Little in Your Life?

As you become aware of Self-Sabotage Strategies, you will be able to spot them in your life and in the lives of your teammates. The next step is to intervene by teaching your people about the importance of raising Deserve Levels... the need for us to get permission from our past... and the need to confront the fears in our lives.

I can't emphasize enough how important it is for you and your people to review your beliefs and identify your Self-Sabotage Strategies

I can't emphasize enough how important it is for you and your people to review your beliefs and identify your Self-Sabotage Strategies so that you give yourself an honest opportunity to be all you can be.

so that you give yourself an honest opportunity to be all you can be.

The key to living your dreams is to raise your Deserve Level and to rid your life of Self-Sabotage Strategies so that you GET — and KEEP — what you deserve in your life and your business.

In closing, here's an anonymous poem that tells you everything you need to know about the power and importance of a high Deserve Level. As you read this, ask yourself , "Am I bargaining for too little in my life?"

I bargained with life for a penny,
Only to learn dismayed,
That any wage I would have asked of life,
Life would have gladly paid.

Balancing on the Emotional Teeter-Totter

*What lies behind us and what lies before us are
tiny matters compared to what lies within us.*

Ralph Waldo Emerson

O ne of the best nuggets of wisdom I've ever
heard comes from Jim Rohn, the much-admired
motivational speaker:

*"Work harder on yourself than you do at your job.
When you work at a job, you'll make a living. When you
work on yourself, you'll make a fortune."*

Working on yourself — that's what this chapter is
about. During my years working with people in Direct
Sales, I've interviewed hundreds of successful leaders
to discover the key to longevity in the business. I've
discovered that the key to success boils down to a **balance** between **challenging yourself...** and **indulging
yourself.** If you go too far in one direction or the other,
you sabotage your success. But when you're in balance

between challenging yourself and indulging yourself, you're **both** *having fun...* **and** *making money.*

How to Know Which Mode You're in

Here's a simple way to define these polar opposites. When you're in the **challenging yourself mode,** you're on high alert. You're wearing your business hat, and you're focused on making things happen and making money. In this mode you stretch, reach, work hard, and focus on growing your organization and grabbing the brass ring. There's a danger, however, in taking

When you're in the challenging yourself mode, you're on high alert.

this mode to an extreme. If you get way out of balance in challenging yourself, you can easily slip into the **Rescuer role,** over-giving to your people and then resenting it. When people talk about being burned out, they're describing a major symptom of being over-challenged.

When you're in the **indulging yourself mode,** you're wearing your relaxation hat. You're focused on kicking back and pampering yourself. In this mode you recharge your batteries by pulling back from work, reading, doing yoga, going on vacation, and taking naps. The indulging yourself mode is necessary to avoid burnout,

When you're in the indulging yourself mode, you're wearing your relaxation hat.

but the danger in staying in this mode too long is that it can become a habit and an excuse for not working. When that happens, people start taking the easy way out. They slip into the **Victim role,** making excuses for their lack of production by blaming the products or the opportunity or their sponsor or anything else they can think of. What they're really saying is they've tipped too far in the direction of the indulging yourself mode, but they don't want to admit it.

Keeping the Teeter-Totter Level

To be successful in the business, you need a healthy tension between both modes. You can't focus on one mode at the expense of the other, which is why the most productive, most fulfilled leaders hold challenges and indulgences in equal measure. When either the "challenging yourself" part or the "indulging yourself" part of the equation remains out of balance for long, then something has to give. And what usually gives is the commitment to the business.

The key to keeping balanced between challenging yourself and indulging yourself is to take little steps between the two so that you avoid tipping too far in one direction.

Maintaining a balance between challenging ourselves and indulging ourselves is easier said than done. As we learned as kids on the playground, it's tough to straddle a teeter-totter by yourself and keep it balanced in the middle. To prevent the teeter-totter from tipping all the way down in one direction, you have to continually make small adjustments in your position.

The same principle applies to your business. The key to keeping balanced between challenging yourself and indulging yourself is to take little steps between the two so that you avoid tipping too far in one direction. Not only do you have to keep *yourself balanced,* but you have to *help your people keep their lives and businesses balanced,* too, or you'll find yourself with fewer and fewer partners in your business.

Symptoms of Over-Challenged and Over-Indulged

When we're in balance, we're in the best position to succeed in life and business. But because balance is not a static state, it's easy to slip off center in one direction or the other. Balance is an **on-going process,** not a destination, which means you have to make continual small adjustments between being over-challenged... and over-indulged.

To stay in balance, we need to be aware of certain symptoms that pop up to warn us that we need to shift our priorities in order to center ourselves. Below is a list of symptoms that tell us when we're out of balance.

Over-Challenged
(over performing)

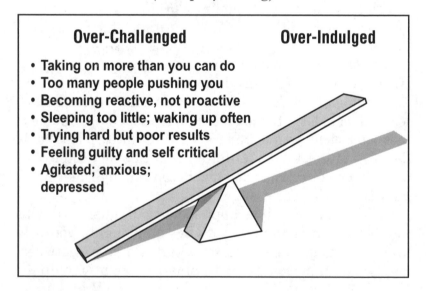

Over-Challenged

- Taking on more than you can do
- Too many people pushing you
- Becoming reactive, not proactive
- Sleeping too little; waking up often
- Trying hard but poor results
- Feeling guilty and self critical
- Agitated; anxious; depressed

Over-Indulged

Over-Indulged
(under performing)

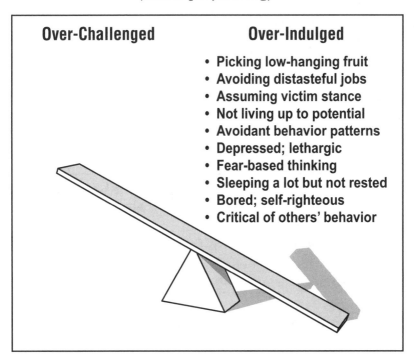

Over-Challenged

Over-Indulged

- Picking low-hanging fruit
- Avoiding distasteful jobs
- Assuming victim stance
- Not living up to potential
- Avoidant behavior patterns
- Depressed; lethargic
- Fear-based thinking
- Sleeping a lot but not rested
- Bored; self-righteous
- Critical of others' behavior

Which teeter-totter best describes where you are in your business at this moment? Are you in the *over-challenged mode,* or are you in the *over-indulged mode?* Take a moment to place yourself on either the **over-indulged** or the **over-challenged** teeter-totter. How about the key people in your organization — can you tell which mode they're in at the moment? Place your key people on the most appropriate teeter-totter.

Think of the teeter-totter illustrations as a simple self-diagnostic tool. By placing yourself and your people on the teeter-totters, you can see at a glance what mode everyone is currently in. The chart at the bottom of the next page shows you the antidotes that will help you and your people get back into balance.

Balance Is a Process, Not an Event

One of the objections I hear from women who are out of balance is they will "make some adjustments when they have time."

Well, I'm here to tell you there's **no benefit in waiting!** If you wait too long to shift your weight on a teeter-totter, you'll end up at the bottom on one side or the other. The key to maintaining balance is to understand where you are on the teeter-totter and then to make the small necessary adjustments *immediately!*

You have three positions on your business teeter-totter. You can be leaning to the **over-challenged side.** You can be leaning to the **over-indulged side.** Or you can be **balanced.**

The easiest position to shift to is the **over-challenged side.** When this happens, you'll feel tired, burned out, and frustrated. Most women tip to this side first.

How to Rebalance the Over-Challenged Mode

Symptoms	Possible Antidotes
• Taking on more than you can do	• Celebrate your achievements
• Too many people pushing you	• Spend time with loved ones
• Becoming reactive, not proactive	• Listen to great music
• Sleeping too little; waking up often	• Rest & resuscitate
• Trying hard but poor results	• Schedule a girl's night out
• Feeling guilty and self critical	• Take a 45-minute walk
• Agitated; anxious; depressed	• Play hooky for the afternoon

When people tip to the **over-indulged side,** they let themselves off the hook too easily, make excuses, avoid the distasteful jobs, and become critical of others.

How to Rebalance the Over-Indulged Mode

Symptoms	Possible Antidotes
• Picking low-hanging fruit	• You lack purpose; Find a mission
• Avoiding distasteful jobs	• Challenge yourself more
• Assuming victim stance	• Set deadlines & higher standards
• Not living up to potential	• Stop making excuses
• Avoidant behavior patterns	• Review goals; list strengths
• Depressed; lethargic	• Take a calculated risk
• Fear-based thinking	• Take bold actions
• Sleeping a lot but not rested	• Take actions that make you
• Bored; self-righteous	feel good
• Critical of other's behavior	• Stay away from sympathizers

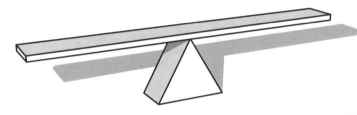

Remember, in this business, you are your own boss. And because you're setting your own goals and working your own plan, it's easy to rationalize taking the afternoon off when you should be on the phone or spending time on projects that take your time but won't make you money.

Successful people **don't confuse activity with productivity.**

Activity is doing things that take time but don't take you to the next level.

Productivity, on the other hand, is doing the things that grow your business or grow your profits.

Successful people don't confuse activity with productivity.

Productivity is time well spent. Activity is simply fiddling while Rome burns. Activity may take up your time, but it's not going to take you where you want to go.

To realize your full potential and to get the most out of the opportunity, you have to stay balanced by constantly taking small steps between challenging yourself and indulging yourself on the teeter-totter of your business. Ironically, in this business, it's the small steps that will make the biggest difference.

CHAPTER EIGHT *8*

Healthful Helping:
Refusing a Ride on
The Rescue Triangle

*All the mistakes I ever made were when I
wanted to say "no" but said "yes" instead.*

Moss Hart
American playwright

*"I*t's better to give than to receive."
You've heard that old expression hundreds of
times, haven't you? Anyone who has seen their children's faces light up as they open their Christmas pres-
ents understands that giving is truly one of the greatest
gifts of all.

That is, as long as it's "healthy giving."

The problem is that some women, u-m-m, make that
the *majority of women,* are super-givers — **Rescuers,**
as I call them — always putting the needs of others
before their own.

In theory, that sounds like a very noble attribute —
sublimating your own wants and needs in order to
help others satisfy theirs. But in truth, giving is like

eating — too much of the wrong stuff leads to an unhealthy lifestyle.

Reserving a Seat on the Rescue Triangle

Relationships are the building blocks in our personal lives, as well as in business. Especially, in this business. When things are going well in our relationships, our lives hum along smoothly, like a limo on the freeway. But when our relationships aren't hitting on all cylinders, then we sputter along, making it hard to steer our lives in the right direction.

Giving is like eating — too much of the wrong stuff leads to an unhealthy lifestyle.

My experience as a therapist has taught me that the single most destructive force that undermines healthy relationships is a dysfunctional communication style I call the **"Rescue Triangle."** This all-too-common psychological dynamic occurs in homes... in marriages... in the workplace... and, most surely, in your business. The Rescue Triangle is a pattern of unhealthy, unproductive role assumptions that keeps all of the participants frustrated and angry.

Here's what the Rescue Triangle looks like:

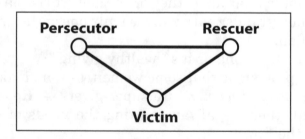

Let's start our discussion by defining each position on the triangle.

Rescuers: Rescuers are people who are over responsible to the needs and wants of others. **Rescuers** give 90% and receive 10% in return. They have a hard time saying "no" to anyone because they don't want to appear selfish. Rescuers see themselves as nurturers and caregivers and derive their self-satisfaction from these roles, but all too often, they subjugate their own needs to others. As a result, Rescuers are reluctant to ask someone to meet their needs, for they think their role in life is to be there for others, ever-ready and ever-responsive.

> *Rescuers are people who are over-responsible to the needs and wants of others.*

Because Rescuers fail to set firm boundaries, others feel they can dump their problems and their work into the Rescuer's lap, which gets fuller as the day grows longer. Because Rescuers think they are *obligated* to help others, they don't think there is an alternative to bailing people out. Often, they give not because they **want to,** but because they think they **should.**

Rescuers tell themselves, "No matter what I feel... what I want... what I need... or what's going on in my life... I have no right to myself. I am here to cater and give to *you.*" Unfortunately, "you" is ultimately everyone but themselves: team members, husband, children, parents, friends, charity, and volunteer organizations.

Victims: Contrasted to Rescuers, who feel over responsible for other people, victims are people who are *under responsible for their actions.* Victims invite, and sometimes DEMAND, that Rescuers direct their lives or swoop in and rescue them from the messes they've created. Victims tend to be passive and lack purpose and direction in life. They tend to be "blamers," avoiding personal responsibility by blaming someone (or something) for their shortcomings and failings. They look to others to make things right and to tidy up their messes. Victims sense they're powerless, unable to create positive outcomes in their lives. Unwilling to step up and take control of their lives, victims expect others to make their lives better (i.e., the government, their mentor, their spouse, etc.). "They made me..." is the victim's most frequent lament.

> *Contrasted to Rescuers, who feel over responsible for other people, victims are people who are under responsible for their actions.*

In truth, we're all victims of circumstances from time to time. Our car battery goes dead, and we have to call a friend to pick us up. If, however, you have a "friend" or relative who constantly complains that life is unfair and her luck is so lousy while singling you out to rescue her from car emergencies... financial emergencies... and emotional emergencies, then rest assured that someone is pulling your Rescuer strings.

Persecutors: Persecutors are people who are angry, frustrated, or fed up with their own lives, so they lash out at others. There are two kinds of Persecutors: **Predisposed** and **Situational.** **Predisposed Persecutors** are rare, but when you deal with one, you know it. Predisposed Persecutors are aggressive, type-A personalities who bully and belittle everyone around them. Men who physically and emotionally abuse their wives and children are classic examples of Predisposed Persecutors.

> *Persecutors are people who are angry, frustrated, or fed up with their own lives, so they lash out at others.*

The other kind of persecutor is a **Situational Persecutor,** which is a role all of us fall into from time to time. When I talk about playing the role of Persecutor in the Rescue Triangle, I'm talking about Situational Persecution. One moment a person is playing the role of the victim, and the next moment they're wearing the Persecutor hat.

Ironically, Persecutors often start out as Rescuers who get fed up and suddenly switch over to the Persecutor's position.

Ironically, Persecutors often start out as Rescuers who get fed up and suddenly switch over to the Persecutor's position. When this happens, the switch is often signaled by language such as, "After all I've done for you, how can you treat me like this? Do you know what your problem is? Your problem is (fill in the blank with a criticism)."

After a while, the Persecutor will feel guilty, and the guilt will build a bridge back to the Rescuer role, and the cycle starts all over again.

Buying a Ticket on the Rescue Triangle Ride

Okay, you've learned about the three roles in the Rescue Triangle. Most likely you've recognized yourself and some of your relationships in these three descriptions.

Now let's take a moment to observe the Rescue Triangle in action in your business. What follows is a typical scenario that happens all too frequently. As you read this, ask yourself if you've ever hitched this ride on the Rescue Triangle.

You sponsor a new person into your business. She's got lots of financial and emotional challenges in her life, but she's fun and full of personality and has what it takes to become a big producer. She's excited about the business, and you're excited about her potential. You have big plans for her future, so you go to special lengths to make sure she succeeds.

The day she signs up, you tie her to your hip. You help her make her list. You train her. You call her twice a day to give her encouragement. You pick her up when her car breaks down. You lend her money to buy product. You listen to her problems and counsel her on how to make things better in her life.

Then one day without warning, she stops taking your calls. You leave messages on her answering machine, but she won't return your calls. She drops off the face of the earth. You bent over backwards for her, and she acts like you don't exist. Exasperated, you say to yourself, "After all I did for her, this is how she treats me? She's got her nerve! I'm tempted to go over to her house and give her a piece of my mind."

Healthful helping means refusing a ride on the Rescue Triangle.

Did you see yourself in this scenario? See how easy it is to start in the **Rescuer** role ("I'll save you")... only to switch to the **Victim** role ("After all I did for her, how can she do this to me?")... and then angrily jump to the **Persecutor** role ("I'd like to give her a piece of my mind.")?

You wanted to help your new recruit. But because you bought a ticket on the Rescue Triangle, it wasn't **healthful helping,** was it? Healthful helping means refusing a ride on the Rescue Triangle.

Two Players, No Winners

The irony of the Rescue Triangle is that every player gets to take a turn at every position. If you play Rescuer long enough, you become a Victim. And when you get fed up enough with either of these two positions, you can explode into the Persecutor position. The participants play musical chairs on the Triangle until someone drops out.

The irony of the Rescue Triangle is that every player gets to take a turn at every position.

How do you break the cycle of the Rescue Triangle? The first step is awareness. Most people "inherit" tickets to the Rescue Triangle by growing up in families that unwittingly played the game. But by being aware of this dysfunctional dynamic, you can take the next step and disengage from the game by refusing to play!

How to Make Your Exit from the Rescue Triangle

Not surprisingly, the vast majority of women spend most of their working hours playing the Rescuer role.

As I said earlier, there's nothing wrong with wanting to help others. That's a very noble sentiment. But in order for your helping to be **healthful,** as opposed to hurtful, you have to disengage yourself from the Triangle.

Think of healthy relationships as a choreographed dance between two graceful partners. You take a step, and the other person reciprocates with a complementary step.

Think of healthy relationships as a choreographed dance between two graceful partners. You take a step, and the other person reciprocates with a complementary step. However, if your partner is taking all the steps, you're not dancing. You're just being pushed and pulled around the floor. Likewise, if you take a step and the other person refuses to take a complementary step, that tells you *they don't really want to dance WITH YOU* — they want you to dance FOR THEM. That's not dancing. That's performing. Healthy relationships are about DANCING TOGETHER, not PERFORMING SOLO!

What follows are four strategies for creating healthy relationships through **healthful helping:**

1) *Resolve not to give more than your fair share.* On occasion, you may need to give more than you get, perhaps 60% "giving" to 40% "getting". But a 90/10 or 80/20 ratio of giving to getting — as many women are accustomed to — is unacceptable.

2) *Ask for people to give back.* This is a tough rule for many women to put into practice. But for a healthy, balanced relationship to take root and grow, you must learn to ask for something in return when you give. Remember: You're not being selfish when you ask — you're being honest! Think of it this way: If you ask for something back and someone won't give it to you, they're telling you they're not interested in a relationship. This axiom applies to your personal life as well as your business life. So stand up and ask!

> *If you ask for something back and someone won't give it to you, they're telling you they're not interested in a relationship.*

3) *Learn to say "no."* Most women are guilty of falling into the habit of saying "yes" when they really want to say "no" because they don't want to disappoint others. Yes, they may not disappoint others, but in the process, they disappoint themselves, which eventually leads to resentment.

If you feel like saying no, say it! You'll feel better and the other person will know where you stand.

4) *Set your boundaries.* You need to know what is acceptable behavior in a relationship and what is unacceptable. Without boundaries, both parties are confused and conflicted. If what is acceptable on a Tuesday is out of bounds on a Wednesday, can you blame the other party for being confused and angry? Set your boundaries — and stick with them!

Reciprocity: A Big Word with Even Bigger Benefits

There you have it — the five keys to **healthful helping**. A reminder: The Rescue Triangle is as prevalent in people's *business lives,* as it is in their personal lives.

I remind you of this because people run their businesses like they run their lives. If they're organized and efficient at home, they'll be organized and efficient in their businesses. Likewise, if the Rescue Triangle is alive and well in their homes, then it will be alive and well in their business relationships.

> *Reciprocity is a fancy term for the Golden Rule.*

It's been my observation that the women who flourish in this business have disengaged themselves from the Rescue Triangle by **demanding reciprocity** in their relationships.

Reciprocity is a fancy term for the Golden Rule: I help you. You help me back. I call you. You call me back. I support you. You support me back. I'm loyal to you. You're loyal to me back. I'm positive and cheerful. You're positive and cheerful back.

The key to reciprocity is to be as respectful and even-handed **to yourself** as you are to others. Giving and receiving in equal measure sounds fair, doesn't it? And it *is* fair. But the only way to make sure the playing field *stays fair* is for you to practice **healthful helping** in every relationship. Every day. In every way.

By setting boundaries in your relationships and sticking to them, you will set the stage for healthy relationships... and a wealthy lifestyle.

Flow: The Marriage of Passion and Purpose

*The world makes way for people
who know where they are going.*

Ralph Waldo Emerson

W e've all experienced those times when we're so totally absorbed in a project that we feel extra alive and time whizzes by so fast that hours seem like minutes.

Psychologists have a term to describe these experiences.

Flow.

When we're experiencing **flow,** work and play become one. We feel empowered. Energized. Stronger. More alert. More focused.

In the words of one best-selling psychotherapist, flow is the "psychology of optimal experience." I have a simpler definition. I call flow "the marriage of passion and purpose."

The Power of Passion and Purpose

When I talk or write about passion and purpose, I always discuss them together because, as the song says, "You can't have one without the other." **Passion** fuels our **purpose,** and purpose gives meaning to our lives. Singly, they can cause more harm than good. Passion without purpose is hedonism. Purpose without passion is tedium.

> *Passion fuels our purpose, and purpose gives meaning to our lives. Singly, they can cause more harm than good. Passion without purpose is hedonism. Purpose without passion is tedium.*

But when passion and purpose marry, the better angels of our nature are set free, and, in their wake, inventions are made... businesses are started... churches are built... people are freed... nations are founded... charities are funded... and the world becomes a better, brighter place.

Let's take a moment to look at the concepts of passion and purpose so that you can better understand how they power your business.

Passion: The Fuel

There are two kinds of passion in people's lives. The first type of passion is the overarching zest for life, what the French call *joie de vivre.*

It's easy to recognize people with *joie de vivre.* They are engaged and excited about life, never bored, always animated, and enjoy every pursuit in their lives. These are people who work hard and play hard... people who never take their health or their blessings for granted... people you'll never hear say, "Thank God it's Friday," because for them, Monday morning at work is just as delightful as Saturday at the beach.

People with *joie de vivre* don't hide from the realities of life. They feel pain. They have fears. But they face their fears, and they persevere in spite of setbacks and hardships, determined to make the best of a bad hand and excited to be sitting at the table long after the cynics and sourpusses have cashed in their chips.

The second type of passion is **focused passion.** People with **focused passion** are single-minded in pursuit of their goal. They stay with a task or commit themselves to a calling with fierce, unilateral determination. People with focused passion are so dialed in that obstacles that would provoke most people to quit are merely speed bumps to them. The epitome of focused passion is Michelangelo lying on his back on rickety scaffolding for 10 hours a day for four years to paint the ceiling of the Sistine Chapel.

People with focused passion are so dialed in that obstacles that would provoke most people to quit are merely speed bumps to them.

I must say that one of the biggest blessings of working with so many business leaders over the years is the opportunity to surround myself with passionate people. I can tell you from experience that passion is essential for success in any endeavor, but most especially in Direct Sales.

The good news is that passion is contagious, so if you've set lofty goals in the business and are serious about reaching them, then make it a point to keep company with your most passionate partners. They'll still be there long after the negative nabobs have faded into the sunset.

Purpose: The Engine

If passion is the fuel of success, then **purpose** is the engine. A person can have all of the passion in the world, but if they don't have an engine to drive them to their destination, their passion is nothing more than a fire hazard just waiting to ignite and burn up their dreams.

If passion is the fuel of success, then purpose is the engine.

When we have purpose in our lives, it means we're doing the right things for the right reasons. Purpose gives our lives meaning and makes us feel valued and important. People who are living a life of purpose love what they do and are good at it.

Steven Covey, author of the multi-million bestseller, *7 Habits of Highly Effective People,* illustrates the power of purpose by asking you to imagine the following situation:

You've been offered a job that pays a million dollars a year. If you take the job, you must agree to work at the job eight hours a day, six days a week, for 40 years. The job is to spend the first four hours of your work day digging a hole and the next four hours filling in that hole. That's all there is to the job. Dig a hole, fill it in, eight hours a day, five days a week, 50 weeks a year, for 40 years.

Would you take the job? The money is great, no argument there. But because **the work would serve no purpose,** how long would it take before you'd hate your job?... hate your life?... and hate yourself? A day? A week? A month? A year? Think about it — the most valuable commodity we have is time, and if you *volunteered* to spend almost 50% of your waking hours performing a passionless task devoid of purpose, could you respect yourself? Could you ever be truly happy? Not a chance.

That's why people who work at jobs they hate in exchange for a paycheck are just chasing after fool's gold. Yes, we all need money to live in this material world. But people who think that money or a "secure job" is fair compensation for working at a job that doesn't give their lives purpose and meaning, well, they're just kidding themselves.

What Is Your Purpose Statement?

When my brother passed away a few years ago, I was devastated. In my grief, I retreated into myself for nearly a year, and part of my healing and coming to terms with my loss was to question the basic assumptions of my life. As you recall, questions like these come up when you're in the **Cocooning** phase of the four **Cycles of Change:**

What is the meaning of life?

What is important?

What has value?

What should I do with the rest of my life?

After much questioning and introspection, I decided to continue my work with Direct Sales professionals, and I formulated the purpose statement that guides me to this day:

My Purpose Statement

To help others to make the kind of choices they need to make in order to feel better about themselves and for me to receive the abundance I deserve.

Notice that there are two big propositions at work in my purpose statement. The first proposition is **giving.**

My purpose is to give my talents and efforts toward *helping others* grow personally and professionally.

> *From a psychological standpoint, giving and receiving are both necessary parts of the Reciprocal Cycle. People who refuse to receive compromise their giving; conversely, people who refuse to give compromise their receiving.*

The second proposition is **receiving.** I'm willing to give, but I will also expect to *receive* something back from that giving. A relationship is a two-way dance of give and take, and if I give expertise and advice that has value, then I expect something of equal value in return.

What about you? Have you written a purpose statement for your life? If you're like most women, your purpose statement will have something to do with giving. The *receiving part* of the purpose statement is where most women fall short. All too often, women feel good about giving, but unworthy of receiving.

From a psychological standpoint, giving and receiving are both necessary parts of the **Reciprocal Cycle**. People who refuse to receive compromise their giving; conversely, people who refuse to give compromise their receiving.

Purpose and Passion in the Party Plan Business Concept

Are you old enough to remember the Certs commercial on TV that touts Certs as "two mints in one" — a breath mint AND a candy mint? Well, in this business, participants get two benefits in one — **passion** AND **purpose.**

Anyone who has ever attended a Party Plan event

will immediately recognize the **passion** the participants have for their products and their opportunity. Where else can you receive hands-on experience with top-of-the-line products in a relaxed, festive environment surrounded by fun-loving people? Answer: You can't. Which is why Direct Sales is growing by leaps and bounds while most retailers are struggling to stay alive in the wake of Wal-Mart's increasing domination.

> *Anyone who has ever attended a Party Plan event will immediately recognize the passion the participants have for their products and their opportunity.*

As for **purpose,** this industry stands alone as a way for people to custom-build their business around their purpose. In a traditional job or career, your employer's purpose supercedes your purpose, so you have to schedule your life around your business obligations.

In this business, it's just the opposite — *you schedule your business around your life!* Always remember — *it's your purpose,* not *someone else's,* that will determine your goals and commitment to the business.

> *As for purpose, this industry stands alone as a way for people to custom-build their business around their purpose.*

Your purpose may be to help others... or to help yourself and your family. The Party Plan concept can do that for you.

Your purpose may be to grow personally... or to grow professionally. The Party Plan concept can do that for you.

Your purpose may be to work part time... or full time. The Party Plan concept can do that for you.

Your purpose may be to earn a little money... or a lot. The Party Plan concept can do that for you.

Your purpose may be to own your own business... or to own your own life. The Party Plan concept can do that for you.

> *Whatever your purpose, the Party Plan business concept can be customized to accommodate your dreams... your goals... your agenda... and your needs.*

Whatever your purpose, the Party Plan business concept can be customized to accommodate your dreams... your goals... your agenda... and your needs. After all, it's your life. It's your business. And it's *your purpose* at stake.

So, if your purpose involves having fun, making money, and making a difference in people's lives, then stay on board the party train... and *Party with a Purpose!*

CONCLUSION

The Parable of the Tiny Acorn

Everything you want in life is on the other side of fear.

Farrah Gray, author
Reallionaire

We're never too old for fairy tales and parables, are we? The message of *Beauty and the Beast,* for example, is just as relevant to us at forty years old, as it was when we were four. What follows is a powerful parable about why, in the end, every important decision in life requires courage... and a leap of faith.

ONCE UPON A TIME there lived a tiny acorn that was determined to become the best acorn she could be. She was smaller than all of the other acorns in the neighborhood, but that only made her more determined to become an Acorn with a "capital A." So, she studied hard at Treetop Prep, graduating with honors and receiving a scholarship to Acorn State, where she majored in botany.

It was during her freshman year in college that a professor said something that would forever change the little acorn's outlook on the world:

"An acorn's purpose," the professor droned, *"is not to remain an acorn but to grow into an oak!"*

Whoa! This bit of information threw the tiny acorn into a tailspin. Up to this point, the tiny acorn had put all her energy into becoming the best at what she was — an acorn. Now, all of a sudden, she was told her potential was much greater than acorn-ness. The little acorn was told she could reach for the heavens and become, gulp, a mighty oak!

> "An acorn's purpose," the professor droned, "is not to remain an acorn but to grow into an oak!"

She peeked upward from the branch where she was hanging and saw hundreds of limbs towering above her.

"I'm supposed to grow into one of THESE?" she whispered to herself. *"Oh, this growing-thing is a scary concept. This will require some research and some serious soul searching."*

So, the tiny acorn read every book and article ever written about oaks. She tuned into OAK-TV every morning and Google-searched OAK on the Internet every night. But the more she learned, the more frightened she became, because it looked like there was no way around her fate. Out of desperation, she sought out the advice of a butterfly and a tree frog.

"Both of you started as something else, and then grew into what you are today," the tiny acorn said. *"Mr. Frog, you were once a tadpole. And Miss Butterfly, you were once a caterpillar. What advice can you give me about growing from an acorn... into an oak?"*

The three of them talked far into the night... and well into the next day. The more the frog and the butterfly talked, the more the tiny acorn understood that the secret to growth couldn't be found in the research (for she had researched until she was brown in the face). And the secret to growth couldn't be found from interviewing others (for she had interviewed every acorn and giant oak and frog and butterfly in the grove).

The secret to growth, the tiny acorn discovered, was this:

You have to let go... before you can grow.

So, with a sigh of resignation and hope in her heart, the little acorn let go... and fell silently to the ground.

Years passed. A towering oak stood sentry over a small clapboard house. One morning a proud father rigged up a rope swing on the lowest limb of the mighty oak. That afternoon, a smiling mother lifted her little girl onto the seat of her new swing. At the child's urging, the mother pushed her daughter high into the air.

> *The secret to growth, the tiny acorn discovered, was this: You have to let go... before you can grow.*

"I want to jump, Mommy," the little girl shouted, *"but I'm scared."*

"At the top of your swing, just let go," the mother reassured the little girl. *"Trust me,"* the mother said softly. *"Once you let go, you'll either land on your feet, or you'll tumble and then jump to your feet. Either way, you'll be okay."*

At the height of her swing, the little girl let go and flew through the air before hitting the ground with a thud and somersaulting onto her back. The little girl giggled with delight as she lay sprawled on her back, squinting at the sunlight breaking through the branches.

"I let go, Mommy, and I flew," the little girl shouted.

And to the laughing little girl... the sunlight winking through the leaves made it look as if the towering oak were laughing right along with her.

You Have to Let Go... in Order to Grow!

Isn't that an enchanting little story? *The Parable of the Tiny Acorn* touches us, but more importantly, it *teaches us* a valuable lesson: In order to grow... in order to reach our full potential... there comes a point when we have to let go of our limiting beliefs and TAKE ACTION!

> *But if you want to grow... if you truly want to reach your fullest potential, then you have to step out and accept challenges, rather than rationalize all of the reasons you should stay rooted to "what I am," instead of committing yourself to "what I could become."*

Although the parable reads like a children's story, it still resonates with meaning for adults because it illustrates a challenge that we all have to deal with all of our lives — fear of the unknown.

When I have clients who are struggling with making big changes in their lives, I tell them that their future happiness will hinge on how they choose to respond to this question:

"Which is stronger — your urge to grow? Or your resistance to change?"

I know from my experience as a therapist, as well as my personal experience, that people resist change. We humans are, after all, creatures of habit, and any deviation from those habits is awkward, at the very least, and often painful.

But if you want to grow... if you truly want to reach your fullest potential, then you have to step out and accept challenges, rather than rationalize all of the reasons you should stay rooted to "what I am," instead of committing yourself to "what I could become."

A Leap of Faith

I made this book as short as possible, knowing that big things can come in small packages. And I truly believe that the information contained in these pages is big enough and powerful enough to change your life for the better, forever!

Let's recap some of the things you've learned:

You've learned about a powerful, growing marketing concept called Party Plan marketing.

You've learned that women are ideally suited to succeed in the business.

You've learned why Gratitude Recruiting is the key to successful recruiting.

You've learned that the secret to retention is helping your people understand the Cycles of Change and survive The Doldrums.

You've learned how to refuse a ride on the Rescue Triangle.

You've learned how to *help others*... without *hurting yourself.*

And you've learned how the combination of purpose and passion can overcome almost any obstacle.

This business gives women the rare opportunity to deal with all of the unfinished emotional issues in their lives... to do well for themselves while doing good for others... and, best of all, to develop their soul in the process.

I hope the psychological secrets you've learned in this book will not only serve you well in Party Plan marketing, but in all of your emotional relationships. This business gives women the rare opportunity to deal with all of the unfinished emotional issues in their lives... to do well for themselves while doing good for others... and, best of all, to develop their soul in the process.

In closing, I hope with all *my* heart that you'll take the tiny acorn's message to *your* heart and *let go* of your preconceived notions... in order *to grow* in your business — and in your life.

Some women will.

Some women won't.

How about you?